PELICAN LATIN AM[ERICAN LIBRARY]
General Editor: Richard

FREEDOM TO ST[ARVE]

CW00690920

'Paul Gallet' is a French priest who insists that his
work and situation are so typical that neither his
name nor that of his town need be mentioned. In
1962 he went to Brazil in answer to the Pope's plea
for more clergy to volunteer to work in Latin
America, where so few priests serve such a large
Catholic population. With a wide experience of
both urban and rural working-class parishes in
France, he expected to encounter familiar problems.
He was unprepared for the kind of poverty he
found in North-East Brazil.

Freedom to Starve

Paul Gallet

With an Introduction by
Michel Quoist and Rosemary Sheed
Translated by Rosemary Sheed

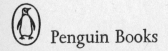 Penguin Books

Penguin Books Ltd, Harmondsworth,
Middlesex, England
Penguin Books Inc., 7110 Ambassador Road,
Baltimore, Maryland 21207, U.S.A.
Penguin Books Australia Ltd, Ringwood,
Victoria, Australia

First published as El Padre by Les Éditions Ouvrières 1967
Published in Great Britain by
Gill & Macmillan Ltd 1970
Published in Pelican Books 1972

Made and printed in Great Britain by
Hazell Watson & Viney Ltd, Aylesbury, Bucks
Set in Linotype Juliana

Introduction

Many people have hazy memories of things they learnt about Brazil in their schooldays – chief products, land area, climate, etc. – and also know perhaps that, unlike the rest of Latin America, Portuguese and not Spanish is the language spoken, which of course is due to a colonial situation that existed long ago before the country achieved its independence. After living and working there for a few years, 'Paul Gallet's' comment might well be 'What independence?'

He himself went to Brazil in 1962, in answer to the Pope's plea, supported by the French bishops, for clergy to volunteer to work in Latin America where some of the largest Catholic populations in the world have the fewest priests to serve them. Having worked in both urban and rural working-class parishes in France, one gets the impression that – apart from the language difference – he did not expect to find anything basically unfamiliar; after all, humanity is the same the world over. He was in for some surprises.

This book is made up of long extracts from his letters – to his parents, family and friends, and some very long ones intended to be reproduced and sent round to former parishioners, mission supporters' groups, etc. – and brief notes from his diaries. It is, therefore, if you like, Brazil through one man's eyes. But one must not say that without immediately making two important points about that one man. First, as he insisted when allowing his letters to be published at all, he is only one of many priests doing similar work, and his situation is so typical and the conditions of his flock so typical that he would allow neither his own name nor that of his town to be mentioned. Any other priest in any other part of north-east Brazil could have written the same book. Well, perhaps; but this seems to me the second point: for all his humility, Paul Gallet is not just *any* priest. No doubt there are many who are equally dedicated, equally compassionate, equally enraged by the poverty and squalor and disease they see around them; but I take leave to doubt that there are many who could convey all this as well as he does. After all, the ability to write well is not one of the essential qualities of the priest; it is, however, highly advantageous to the would-be communicator. And what Paul does here is to communicate vividly and directly the experiences of a priest in a situation that will be unfamiliar to most English-speaking readers, though it is horribly familiar to two-thirds of the world. This is not fine descriptive writing; it is straightforward reporting of things heard and seen and done, not with publication in view, but simply to let his friends know what life is like in Brazil, to arouse their compassion and indignation, and ask for their help. But the help he wants is not handouts to 'the poor' – he wants help in changing the situation, in enabling the people he is with, who from years of destitution and hopelessness have become resigned to the sub-human conditions they are living in, to discover their human potential, to stand together as men and fight for recognition as such.

'The first task,' he says, 'is not to fill our church or get people to the sacraments, but to create, or help to form, natural communities among them. How can you preach about what the gospel teaches, or about heaven and hell, to people living in sub-human conditions? What right have we to try to stick the supernatural on top of a nature that is almost non-existent?' Faced with the imperialist capitalism of the USA, the greed of the rich minority in Brazil, and the

6

corruption that exists at every level of officialdom (even down to a doctor making a woman pay for medicine marked 'free sample' because he knew she couldn't read!), it is no use hoping and praying that things will improve. Still worse is the fatalism of so many of the poorest who feel either that it is 'God's will', or it is just 'Fate', and that it is no use even hoping or praying for any improvement. What is needed is action, and it must be action by the people themselves.

He realized in theory before he went that there was poverty in Brazil; well of course we all know that. Also that there is wealth, and, as in many other places, it is appallingly unevenly distributed. But it was not until he was actually living in the midst of it that the reality of it hit him, and it is that reality he wants to get across to us through this book. As he says, he suddenly realized that the people he had thought of as poor in France would count as very well off indeed in Brazil: to have regular work at all is the exception rather than the rule, and the official minimum wage (which is also normally the maximum) is something under a dollar a day. Life expectancy in north-east Brazil is twenty-seven years, and a man of forty is old there. No one buys milk – it costs too much. The staple diet is cassava flour which fills you up but has almost no nutritive value. Of the school-age population only half go to school at all, and of those only about one in ten finishes primary school. Such facts as these form the skeleton of Paul's story, but he clothes it with the flesh of intensely moving descriptions of people and families, of people with leprosy and TB, families whose houses collapse leaving them homeless as well as penniless; inspiring accounts of things achieved by neighbourly support, or by people working together for something they all need, of sudden discoveries people will make of their capabilities as human beings; and alongside it all the hectic gaiety and noise of Brazilian life, with festivals, religious and otherwise, sometimes inextricably mixed, even the wild celebrations that go

7

on at a funeral, and always, and everywhere, music and dancing.

When you have read this book, you feel as though you have really visited Brazil – the rich industrial south, some of the loveliest country in the world (though only for a visit) and the north-east with its urban and rural poverty – and got to know the people of this astonishing country.

But, perhaps more importantly, you have also received a lot of new insights into what the Church is, what being a priest is. Women with children to support and no husbands frequently become prostitutes; one told Paul that she prayed to our Lady to send her customers; he now understands what our Lord meant by saying that the harlots might go into heaven before the rest of us. He describes an incident when a woman needed a blood-transfusion and had no money to pay for blood, so he and his fellow-priest in the parish gave some and various others did the same, raging over the suggestion that blood must be 'bought'; he even managed to get a chit entitling her to free blood, which he foolishly handed over to the doctor, and never saw again. He goes on: 'Oddly enough, it was just about that time we three decided to stop taking "mass-offerings" . . . Christ's blood isn't bought or sold either.' The poverty he sees around him causes him to reflect on the danger of labelling as a communist anyone who attacks the 'established *dis*order', and on the fact that religion may become an easy way out; church-going may dispense us from effective love of neighbour; one may recall Christ saying that not everyone who says 'Lord, Lord!' will get into heaven.

It is clear that many of the clergy in Brazil feel as Paul does. Towards the end of the book he quotes some fairly startling comments from religious sources. His own diocesan radio station, for instance, marked Independence Day by a programme which included such statements as this: 'Can one talk of independence in a country where more than thirty

million people are starving? Have we any right to do so? ...
We, like all the Brazilians in the underdeveloped areas and
the "marginal" states, we who live in the condition of *non-men* and *sub-men*; it is up to us to transform Brazil into an
independent country!' And the bishop: 'Let us be under no
illusion. Brazil has yet to become independent. The independence which was achieved ... was only independence from
Portugal. In the interim, other nations have appeared to
replace the Portuguese as exploiters. We are still being exploited and sucked dry by other countries.' And another
bishop: 'The courage of the little island of Cuba can be our
symbol and our hope. ... All the aid from rich countries to
our people will never counterbalance the money stolen from
us by the continual depreciation of our raw materials and the
flight of capital.'

Though the picture of poverty, of resignation to poverty,
of government inaction in the face of poverty, is a pretty depressing one, yet, I think we can feel, as Paul himself does, a
certain sense of hope. Two kinds of hope really. First, a hope
that the people of the poor countries will really rise up as
fully human beings and fight for their rights and human
dignity; and second, a new kind of hope for the Church. For
so long in the west the Church has been a rich man's Church,
has sided with the powers-that-be (or at least compromised
with them) and has wherever possible supported the status
quo; now in Brazil and other parts of Latin America it is at
last attacking the corruption of the rich and powerful and
siding with the poor – at last really acting as Christ did –
driving the money-changers out of the Temple, and refusing
to rest content with saying 'Lord, Lord!' – even in the
vernacular.

MICHEL QUOIST AND ROSEMARY SHEED

Part 1
I shall arrive as a poor man

On board the Provence
27 September 1962

LETTER

To his parents: I hope to post this when we land at Recife, which will be on Sunday morning, so that you get some news of me before I write from Rio. I am thinking of you all, and especially of Marie-Lou. How's the work going?

I am going to change now for the games that are being organized on deck to celebrate 'crossing the line'. This voyage is terrific. I feel great, ready to set out for whatever new horizons Christ is leading me to. Brazil is getting very close. A whole new field of action is opening up. I feel stripped of everything; the break will be complete. All the habits of the past are gone. I shall arrive as a poor man, my hands empty, but my heart light and free and so full of love that it feels as though it will burst.

29 September 1962

... When I think that a year ago I was listening to the cows mooing at la Bastelle! * How far off it all seems. Yet how thankful I am to God for the special graces of those times – la Minotière and the working-class world, la Bastelle and the life of the country. Together with Brazil they form a unity in my priestly awareness.

Yves † and I have just been saying our office together, looking out to sea; we then clambered to the very end of the prow, and said the rosary there in Portuguese. The ship is rushing

* La Bastelle, la Minotière and Chesne-les-Monts are the names given to the parishes where the author worked in France before going to Brazil.

† Yves Laubier is another French missionary priest who went to Brazil with the author and worked with him there. Later they were joined by a third, Richard Desvilles.

13

forward gloriously, pushing on like a wild thing, but with a constant fidelity to her as yet invisible goal, a goal beyond the horizon, which she seems to be pursuing almost as though she were too much in love with it to think what she is doing.

My dear parents, I'm afraid you have sometimes thought me obstinate in my obsession with South America – which is at last close at hand. But the straight line which has led me from the cows of la Bastelle to the shanty-towns of Rio, or the tropical beauty of S., is not simply a yielding to the natural whims of an adventurous temperament. No, that absolutely straight line is of the Lord's making. And if I have not wavered a hair's breadth from it, it is no thanks to *my* purpose or *my* courage, or anything else of my own. It is simply that the Lord made me hear his call, and has filled my heart with infinite love and joy. I don't think a priest's life makes sense apart from love. Thank you for being the first to start me off on the apprenticeship of love – an apprenticeship that ends only with death.

I'll write soon again.

Between Recife and Rio
1 October 1962

LETTER

To his former parishioners and friends: We got back out to sea yesterday evening, having at last touched Brazilian soil. I don't know how to describe what I felt at this first contact. It was like a kick in the stomach – suddenly a whole world of imaginings became a reality. I felt that from having been up to then a disinterested spectator, I was being pushed from behind right out to the middle of the stage. Brazil used to be a name to conjure with, a land of magic. The myth has gone, but something warm has come to stay in my heart. There are faces now. What were just 'problems' have taken on flesh and blood. When I say the myth has gone, what I mean is that the

14

'legend' of Latin America has become a reality. But at the same time, I feel that my enthusiasm has gained new impetus. The long-awaited meeting was no disappointment, more, I imagine, like getting married after only being engaged.

We came into Recife about seven in the morning and went ashore at about eight (it took a while to get through all the formalities of police, customs, etc.). For the morning, Yves and I joined forces with a young married couple, Germans. Since they knew no French and we no German, we spoke Portuguese. We shared a taxi to go round the town and the surrounding countryside. The taxi was a real poem: an ancient Chevrolet, sweating and puffing, with a horn that suddenly started hooting and couldn't be stopped. We went along the main streets of the town, visited some nearby beaches, and then out as far as the town of Olinda, quite near Recife, built long ago by the Dutch.

We went into a church on the hill of San Antonio – a glory of gold and blue ceramic (*azulejos*) standing out against the surrounding dirt and poverty. A small boy reeled off a whole lot of information about it that he obviously knew by heart, and there was a seething mass of kids to encourage him when he asked for money.

It's now fifteen days since I left home, and how long ago it seems! I find it quite hard to think back – all my energies are directed to what lies ahead. To Christ. To other people waiting to be loved. To the immense work, and the immense love I must put into it. I feel overflowing with an irrepressible joy – sometimes I feel I must absolutely shout for joy. I'm on the right road, of that I'm quite sure.

Rio de Janeiro
8 October 1962

LETTER
To his parents and friends: I know you are longing to hear my news, and my first impressions. And I too am equally anxious

15

to get in touch with all of you; you have shown me so much sympathy and affection from the moment you heard of my leaving for Brazil in response to the Pope's call.

How good the Lord is ! My heart is bursting with joy as I write. Yves and I have been in Rio almost a week, and we have already felt the hand of God helping us in a thousand ways, with infinite loving care...

We left Marseilles, aboard the *Provence*, on 20 September, and had a splendid voyage with 1,500 passengers, mostly Italian, Spanish and Portuguese emigrating to Brazil, Argentina or Uruguay, and Brazilians going home. Shipboard life was easy-going and friendly, and, with the peace of the ocean about us, we were able to begin through friendship to make some approach to the thoughts and feelings of Brazil, and the language too (which is, as you probably know, Portuguese). We had long talks with João, our cabin-mate, a young journalist from Rio, and also with his fiancée Jeanne, who works in a shanty-town, and knows the north-east (where we are going) very well. There was also a nun from the state of Paraïba (in the north-east), and a Benedictine priest from Bahia, who sat with us at meals, and helped us with our Portuguese. There was Heinz, a German student from Freiburg University, who was on his way back to Recife for the third time to work on an economics thesis on the situation in the north-east and what the Church is doing about it... We met quite a number of Brazilians, and two priests, who came aboard at Lisbon, became our greatest friends : Padre Zelio and Padre Mateus.

We put in at Barcelona and Lisbon, but had the thrill of touching Brazilian soil for the first time at Recife... It was our first contact with north-eastern Brazil where the Lord is sending us (S. is not far from Recife); our first contact with the charm of the ordinary people of Brazil, with the extreme poverty which is, alas, the chief characteristic of the area, and with their customs. I can't get out of my mind the memory of a poor man bent over a puddle of water in the road, trying to wash his wretched rag of a shirt – alongside great modern blocks of flats. . .

It is extremely hot (October is spring here), and our clerical suits are stifling. Rio at last. . . On 3 October we got up very early, said mass, and then, leaning over the rail of the upper deck, our hearts too full to speak, we watched as the ship sailed into this magnificent bay – it must be one of the most beautiful in the world – Copacabana, with the Sugar-loaf, the Christ of Corcovado, the show of skyscrapers standing out against a background still magnificently wild, a Hollywood décor. . .

We disembarked . . . welcomed with open arms by the (French) Assumptionist Fathers with whom we are to spend a month before we go to Petrópolis. . . Two days of rushing about to register with the French embassy, the Brazilian police and the customs. Luckily (since it is all so complicated that it could have taken far longer), we were told what to do, and piloted from one office to another by Brother Jacques, and our friend Padre Zelio. The operation concluded with *thirty-three* sets of our fingerprints being made – our fingers first generously blackened by an official with an inky roller. Time doesn't matter in Brazil, and these two days were certainly useful in helping us to get rid of our European habit of always being in a hurry. . .

We are lucky enough to have a free month in Rio, before we go for our training to Petrópolis; the course begins on 9 November. It will help us to get to know Brazil, and we shall follow up every likely contact. We saw the sights of Rio with Padre Zelio, the Brazilian priest. We went up the Sugar-loaf, to the Christ of Corcovado which dominates the town; we even got as far as the island of Paqueta, and above all, we have begun to get to know the people. Yesterday we spent the whole morning in the shanty-town of Catumbi, where the La Salette Fathers have done tremendous work. In the evening

17

we went to another shanty-town, where Fr Coux is working; there was mass out of doors, and the atmosphere was quite unlike anything I've known before. After mass we had the pleasure of sharing a typically Brazilian meal (rice and black beans) with a local family, in their tiny, flimsy home. They welcomed us with a kindness that was very reminiscent of the working-class families in la Minotière.

The shanty-towns leaning up against the mountains of Rio are a challenge presented by utter poverty to the proud dwellings alongside them... Zelio pointed out how often foreigners 'passing through' Rio give a very false impression when they write about it – they see only the 'beauty', or only the 'ugliness', whereas in fact both are mixed inextricably. We have been deeply touched to see the extent of human warmth and solidarity, and of what can actually be achieved by common effort, in the shanty-towns ... all greatly assisted by the presence of active Christians, YCW members,* the Little Sisters of Père de Foucauld, and some remarkable priests who really do live close to their people.

To Yves and me, yesterday seemed a call from the Lord, and a 'sign' to remind us that he has brought us to Brazil and sent us to the north-east chiefly so as to go to 'the poorest, the little ones' ... We are longing to get to them, to be able to see Christ's face in theirs. We are longing to love them – that is why we are priests. We really are *burning* to get there.

What has struck us most since we got here is the almost total absence of racial prejudice. Everyday life gives continual examples of a tremendously attractive mixture of civilizations, colours and outlooks. There certainly is 'inter-breeding', as we have been told in France, and it is something which could well be a basis for a whole new dimension of Christian

* Young Christian Workers, founded in Belgium in the twenties by Fr Cardjin in order to make Christianity a reality among the workers.

values. Certainly the Negroes predominate in the lower types of work, but in fact, in the street, the shops, the buses, you would hardly be aware of any differentiation, or see the smallest signs of superiority or inferiority. The descendants of Negroes, whites and Indians are stirred together as in a stewpot to make up the one family of Brazilians; and they all seem equally attached to that family, with great ambitions for it, great courage, certain weaknesses and an awareness of the difficulties to be overcome – but that is another subject. There are hideous contrasts in Brazil, and especially in the standards of living. But it seems to be an economic, social and cultural problem, not a racial one... However, I mustn't start forming judgements quite so soon !

There is a lot more I should like to tell you, but it is very late and I must stop, for tomorrow we have to make an early start to São Paulo. Thank you for being with us in your thoughts, and even more in your prayers. May the Lord help us all to answer his call generously, without hesitation or reserve – and above all, joyfully !

It is that joy that I ask him to pass on to you, for one can do nothing without joy – which really means, I suppose, without faith.

Rio de Janeiro
30 October 1962

LETTER
To his parents: Our stay in Rio is coming to an end. Personally I feel happy that our training period is to begin, because it will undoubtedly be both interesting and useful, and I am getting impatient to get to our real journey's end, the northeast. I want to get my roots down in the land the Lord is sending me to.

Yesterday we got a letter from Rome which gave us great joy. Our bishops (Yves's and mine) have met Bishop Riobé as well as the Archbishop and the auxiliary Bishop of S.: they were able to discuss ways and means of setting us to work in the north-east, a providential meeting indeed. We feel more and more pleased to be going to north-eastern Brazil, for that is where there is the most crying need. Our being directed there by the French Committee * is truly providential (they have just confirmed that I am personally to be put in touch with Dom Poletta †) ...

Cuba ... the referendum ... All this is the backcloth to what is happening, in France as here ... only here the overtones are different. The bookies are getting busy, and odds are quietly being laid. But as well as the humorous side there is a tragic one – poverty, hunger, unemployment, the unequal distribution of wealth, the selfishness of the secure. The mixture is explosive – the only question is who will put the first match to it. Are there enough Christians with the courage to set off the revolution of the gospel, the revolution of love?

This must be all for today, with much love; but I am not leaving you, for I really feel there is no distance between us.

Rio de Janeiro
6 November 1962

LETTER
To his family and friends: I am taking advantage of some free time to send you some news of myself. The day after tomorrow I shall at last leave Rio for Petrópolis, where Yves and I will share a period of intensive training (studying Portuguese, and being initiated into the economic, social and

* This is a committee set up, in response to the appeal by Pope John XXIII and Pope Paul VI for more missionaries, to make the necessary practical arrangements for posting French missionary priests to South America.

† Dom, as used here and throughout these letters, is roughly the Portuguese equivalent of Mgr, an honorific title used for prelates.

human problems of Brazil, the problems faced by the Church – we shall do short spells of parish work and write reports about it – and the adjustment of our culture to Brazilian culture, etc.). The work will certainly be very difficult, but also useful and probably exciting. We shall be thirty : priests, religious and laymen from all over the world (only three French).

I have now been in Brazil over a month, and made a fantastic number of contacts and discoveries. Both Yves and I, far from regretting having arrived so long before our course begins, have found this period of 'field-studies' invaluable. It has given us the beginnings of a personal knowledge of this country to which the Lord has sent us – and that is something for which there can be no substitute.

We have got in touch with several communities of priests : two French Brothers of Charity at Santo André, two Canadians at Tucuravi, five or six La Salette Fathers, all Brazilians, at Santa Ana. They all welcomed us with open arms, and we were able to talk to them, and see something of their problems.

We made a coach-trip (seven and a half hours) to São Paulo and what a terrific place it is ! ... It's a hive of activity, with industry starting up everywhere, the fastest growing city in the world (in 1950 one and a half million inhabitants – in 1962 four million). It is now about twenty miles in diameter.

I had the luck to meet a French couple – Jean Tenor, and his wife Sylvie, who have been here six months with Ad Lucem (an organization which trains lay Christians and sends them to work in the Third World).

From São Paulo, we made a detour to Santos, which is the city's port. We spent two days with a 'typically Brazilian' family, our hostess being the sister of our great friend the Brazilian priest we met on the boat. Afterwards, in Rio, we were able to have long talks with the national chaplain of the Brazilian YCW, who told us how delighted he was to see us going off to the north-east where the need is so great. He told us (as Bishop Benelli, the apostolic nuncio, was to confirm) that the north and north-east of Brazil which are the poorest areas in human terms are, alas, the poorest spiritually as well. A lot of religious congregations send priests to the São Paulo area – where they are needed too – but very few send any to the north or north-east, with the result that there are now more priests for the four million people in São Paulo than for the whole of the north and north-east with their twenty-two million.

We then had the extraordinary luck to get two free air trips – return tickets – from Brazilian Pan-Air, from Rio to Brasília (over 800 miles, a two-hour flight).

Brasília shows a totally different aspect of Brazil – ultramodern, young and tough. In three years a capital city has risen up out of the ground, in the middle of the desert. It is a real act of faith, a bet on the future. We met a French priest, Fr Louvier, who had been there a year, and visited his parish in the new city and another parish he looks after which is fifteen miles out of Brasília in the satellite town of Taguatinga – which looks more like a small town in a western than anything else. The apostolic needs are tremendous: you feel what marvellous people they are, how much they could do, and how badly they need God. They are hungry, but there are no priests to give them food.

Back in Rio, a long telephone call from Mgr Illich, the founder of the training centre in Petrópolis. He is a man who really sparkles with intelligence, and has made us more than ever aware of the catholic – i.e. universal – aspect of our coming. I must also mention our visit to the shanty-town of Leme, where a Frenchwoman, Renée, is doing great work; it is right next to Copacabana, so you see minute hovels with whole families living in them a stone's throw from luxury flats, where a family will have twenty-two rooms and perhaps four *empregadas* (maids). There are about 35,000 *empregadas*, nearly all Negro, working in Copacabana.

We met two more French priests: one has been in Brazil a year, and is doing great things in the minor seminary at Bara do Pirai (fifty miles out of Rio); the other, Padre Paolo, is the parish priest of São Mateus, a working-class suburb of Rio. He was deported from Vietnam, and asked to come to Brazil to work. We spent three days in close contact with him, lodging locally, and found them enormously rewarding. Everywhere you find this spiritual hunger, this expectation, this generosity which seems to be simply waiting for the chance to give itself to God. But there are so few priests, and they have to do everything at once – catechizing, starting active lay groups, getting in touch with ordinary people.

All night I kept being woken up by the hypnotic rhythm of the *Macumba*.* The *Macumba* is still very much alive, and there are innumerable other sects too. You remember how we couldn't get real sugar during the war, and everyone tried to get their hands on some saccharine instead? That's really what is happening in Brazil.

Finally, last week we had another trip to São Paulo. The second national congress of the Brazilian ACO † was going on there, and Padre Paolo, the national chaplain, invited us to it. Our days were packed with valuable meetings. I was pleasantly surprised to find that I could follow the lectures and discussions pretty well, despite my poor Portuguese. But heavens, what problems and sufferings the Brazilian working classes face! The minimum official monthly wage in Brazil is

* *Macumba* is the name of a set of religious beliefs and practices originating in Africa but still fairly widespread among the Negroes in Brazil. Its chief characteristic is a kind of pagan spiritualism.

† This is a Catholic workers' association, Acción Católica Operaria, a branch of official Catholic Action. Broadly speaking its aim is to bring Christian principles to bear in the life and conditions of the workers; it has a similar scope to that of the YCW but its members are older.

ridiculously low and even with overtime few workers get enough to support themselves and their families. There are no family allowances, no paid holidays, though a few generous factories do give a small child allowance and sometimes they also pay a small allowance to non-working mothers, but even then, all this means in practice is that a man with a wife and eight children will get enough in allowances to pay for one gallon of milk a month !

This congress was evidence of a young and vigorous ACO, thriving despite all the difficulties.

We were especially struck by how strongly the Brazilians feel about agrarian reform. It's rather as we in France felt about Algeria a couple of years ago. The ACO is the hope for the future of Brazil – and of the Church too, I am sure. Their members are quite as enthusiastic as ours at home, and the battle they have to fight is far harder. There is corruption and bribery everywhere : in the unions, in the press, among police, politicians, and even, I'm sorry to say, ecclesiastics. There is one Christian-based union which has only recently started and is growing fast : the National Workers' Front. There are some courageous bishops and priests, but the whole structure of work and employment is still almost feudal. If you realize that three-quarters of all Brazilians are illiterate, and that only those who read and write (the privileged, in other words) can vote, then you can see the crux of the matter : those who work, who suffer, who are dying of hunger, have no voice.

After the congress closed, about half of the 120 ACO members went to talk to the strikers at a cement factory twenty miles out of São Paulo, at Perus, a working-class development stuck out in the middle of forest-land. 1,200 workers have been on strike for six months, and the boss doesn't really mind because he personally owns thirty-five factories. But the working people are wonderfully courageous and determined, and the National Front are bringing the matter to court. The boss has bought the police and the press (not a single newspaper has mentioned the strike). He has got himself elected a federal deputy largely by threatening to close down factories. The parish priest of Perus was driven out of his house by the police because he was on the side of justice ! Whereupon the workers at once set about building him a little presbytery beside the church.

When we arrived, the priest had got his microphone fixed up in a hut at the top of the hill, and they held an impromptu meeting there. The atmosphere was extraordinary: the priests who had come were cheered; the ACO members spoke. The delegate from the factory, an enormous, athletic-looking Negro, had tears in his eyes. They even called up to the platform the 'two French priests', and we got a great ovation. Yves and I were in white shirts and trousers, but were recognized at once, for these people are well aware that what makes a man a priest is not what he wears but the quality of his love; and while they cheered us, we thought of all the people, poor, humiliated, defeated in life's struggle, who are waiting for us in the north-east.

A woman member also spoke to the strikers' wives, and some young people sang the Brazilian song, 'Worker, be proud'. Then the parish priest ended the meeting with some thoughts on the Magnificat: 'He has put down the mighty from their thrones and exalted those of low degree.' (Can you imagine that happening in France !) A great burst of cheering greeted this gospel message. What struck us most was the determination of these workers to strike peacefully, and not give way to provocation or violence.

When our coach left the village the whole population, men, women and children, gathered on the hillside to let us know how pleased they were with our visit. Their shouts were an echo of all Brazil, and probably of all South America. A shout of joy, anguish, distress, hope, hunger – a call, really: the call of God. But who will hear it?

Dear family and friends, I conclude this letter by passing on this cry, this call, to your hearts, to your thoughts and to your prayers. Some people are frightened, and say 'There will be an explosion.' But Christians mustn't be frightened; they must have the courage to say 'There *must* be an explosion.' We have the Council. The new wine is bubbling up on all sides, and the old bottles will burst. We must jump boldly into this great current of life and youth in the Church. We must pray hard for the Council. Perhaps we could each meditate in our own way on this statement (from a leaflet by one of the Perus strikers): *Deus tarda mas nao falta* – which means 'God is slow, but he never fails us' – he always answers in the end.

Petrópolis
15 November 1962

LETTER

To his family: Mother is quite, quite wrong in thinking that I am having a rest here during this training period. From eight o'clock to half past three we are performing an almost unbroken series of rapid gymnastic feats – with our minds, our memories and our mouths. Sometimes after two, three or four hours of Portuguese, after going over and over the same syllables and phrases, I cannot help starting to laugh – my self-control just goes. Yves and Alain, the Canadian, do just the same. At the moment our teacher is Dona Luisa, a very nice intelligent girl; we call her Dona Machine-gun, and become quite hypnotized by her rhythmic repetition: *Repita, outra vez; traduze, fances-portugues* – which means 'Again, once more, translate, French, Portuguese.' It's wonderful to be a small boy again; it does one good. It teaches one something about sanctity as well as Portuguese. It can't be easy for a young girl to be schoolmarm to three priests aged twenty-seven, thirty-three and thirty-eight. There are twelve teachers in all, for thirty of us. All of them are about twenty, and each week they change. This morning Yves has been 'kept in': he has to go to a special lesson for those who haven't done too well. I'm very proud of not having to be there!

As you might guess, the easiest part for me is the accent. I like the method they are using, though it is hard work. It should be pretty effective. In three weeks we shall be required to speak Portuguese amongst ourselves until two o'clock every day, later on until eight in the evening. At the moment we get on as best we can: some have a bit of English which has somehow stuck in the back of their minds, and others manage to stumble out a few words of French.

I am very pleased to be doing this course. In any case, since I've been asked to, it is clearly the Lord's will. The best thing is to enter into the fun of the thing, keep your feet on the ground, and keep your sense of humour. I'm certainly getting a lot of fun out of it. As Yves says, 'We aren't paid much, but we do enjoy ourselves.' There's one enormous American fellow, and I only wish you could hear him laugh – it's beautiful, almost like a child's laugh, and so absolutely natural that no one can help liking him.

The most important, but also the hardest, thing in studying a language is to discover and gradually become familiar with certain basic sounds which are quite foreign to you because they simply don't exist in your native language: for instance a whole range of As, Es and Os, and a number of syllables which your mouth can't get round at all at first. You need great patience; and it's a great help to be able, at any minute of the day, to draw strength from something inside oneself – and also to be able to laugh at oneself, almost the most important thing of all. The saints always had a sense of humour, and the longer I live the more it seems to me to be the one really essential thing. It stops you from being deceived by appearances. I often think of the words on Newman's tomb: *De imaginibus et fantasmatibus ad veritatem et lucem,* 'I have now passed from the world of appearances, figures and outward forms, to the world of pure truth and total light.'

Well, I must stop, I've rambled on for long enough. I hope you are all well, and my greetings to everyone.

Petrópolis
16 December 1962

LETTER

To his family and friends: I suppose Christmas will be over by the time you get this. But I still want to say Happy Christmas to you all. Christmas in France, Christmas in Brazil (though here it's called Natal, the birth). The problem is whether we are sufficiently childlike to receive Christ; sufficiently poor to have anything to give; sufficiently foolish to be able to love.

We have been here since 8 November, Yves and I. Petrópolis is a very pretty little town, nearly 3,000 feet above sea level, with mountains all round. Though we're only about twenty miles from Rio, it is much cooler here (summer is just starting).

There are twenty-five of us on this course: three lay Americans and Canadians, nine American priests, three Irish, one Canadian and two French – ourselves; also seven American nuns. Our community, as you can see, really represents the catholicity of the Church! For us it is a wonderful opportunity for enrichment – both human and spiritual. The work is hard, but very exciting. Here is a rough timetable of our day: mass at six; a lecture at eight; from nine until one we do Portuguese (with four breaks of a few minutes each). At one, lunch; at two, back to Portuguese until three thirty. After that we each do our own work – every week we have to write an account of two things we have read. At six, an hour in the chapel – and on Fridays, a community mass. At seven, supper, known here as *jantar*. At eight, another lecture, or group discussions. Finally, before we go to bed, we meet at about nine-thirty for 'beer' – in other words, a drink and a bit of relaxation together. It's then that we have our best laughs and also our most exciting discussions, for this is when we try to work things out together...

The method used in our language classes is based on the principle that 'habit is second nature'. The object is to give us 'super-memorization', especially of phonetics. Gradually the ear becomes attuned, and that is the most important part – vocabulary can always be picked up later. This method gives you a firm basis – and, as a bonus, it is very useful from the spiritual point of view too: you are forced to be 'poor in spirit' when you are in constant contact with a girl of twenty who has everything to teach, and you know nothing. For a priest this is a tremendous grace, and what an excellent preparation for our mission! After all, the most important thing for us when we arrive in Brazil is to get rid of any sense of superiority.

But we are getting, as well as a knowledge of the language, a thorough spiritual and methodological training: lectures in geography (peoples, not rainfall), sociology, economics, the religious problems in Latin America, and so on. The two most important things are our eucharistic life (for only Christ himself can teach us real poverty) and our community life (for only together can we learn to love). The focal point of each day is our hour with the Lord; and the focal point of each week is the community mass on Friday evening, at which a lot of priests communicate rather than each saying his own mass.*

We spend the weekends in parishes, going off separately either to Rio or somewhere else in the area; and this contact with different priests and different forms of parish life is also

---

* At that date concelebration had not as yet been re-established.

very interesting. I am beginning to baptize and even hear confessions in Portuguese.

One small story in conclusion. The other Sunday I spent the afternoon in the botanical gardens in Rio with a student. We talked about Brazil and about the poverty and injustice which are the daily bread of its people. He said, 'My father is an active Communist; he is a lawyer, and stood in the elections. I respect his ideals, but for me there is a higher ideal in the gospel and the Church's social teaching. But what is so tragic in Brazil is that we haven't enough priests to make it known, and since you must have *some* ideal to fight poverty with, they look for one elsewhere.' . . . As one active Christian in Brasília said to me: 'A revolution in Brazil is both necessary and inevitable. The only question is whether it will be carried out by Christians or against them.' Only God can help us; only his love can break through our shell of selfishness!

Belo Horizonte
31 December 1962

LETTER

To his family: Tomorrow it'll be 1963. . . Happy New Year to you all. Though I'm not with you in body, I am in spirit. . . Thank you for your good wishes (which I haven't received yet). I know the Lord will pay you a hundredfold for the sacrifice you have made in letting me go. Thank you for the books (they haven't arrived yet, but they will).

We left Petrópolis last Friday, and we are free until next Sunday – nine days' holiday. It's great, and indeed we need it to get our breath. I've come to Belo Horizonte, a town in the interior (you can see it on the map between Rio and Brasília) with Yves and Bill, an American from Buffalo. We got on the coach at ten in the evening, and arrived at seven thirty next morning. We are staying with the Franciscans who have a college here.

Belo Horizonte is a fine city with 900,000 people, and definitely 'of the interior' in its way of life. It is the capital of Minas Gerais, and shows us yet another aspect of the country.

Yesterday we went to see another very typical town, about fifty-five miles from here, Ouro Prêto (means 'Negro gold') – a gold-(and diamond-)rush town of seventy or eighty years ago. It's a strange, museum-like town, with hundreds of steeples. The churches are typically baroque in style, with very luscious fleshly statues of Our Lady, which are surprising, to say the least, but they are a good image of Brazil too. In the intermingling of blacks, Indians and whites, pagan elements have got mixed in with Christian, especially during the colonial period which marked the high point of the *fazendas* (large farming settlements) and the development of the sugar industry. It would take a book to explain the whole thing. Really you have to be here to begin to understand the historical background, and without that you could never understand what's going on now. That is another reason why these journeys are so interesting to us, to help get inside the skin of Brazil. You can't compare Brazil with France – only with Brazil.

Petrópolis
Ash Wednesday, 27 February 1963

LETTER
To his parents: This will be my last letter from Petrópolis. Tomorrow we'll say our farewells after a community mass in the morning, and shall scatter to the four corners of Brazil: Goias, São Paulo, Minas Gerais, Natal, Maranhao, etc. It will be a sad moment; you don't spend four months together without becoming friends. I shouldn't be surprised if there are tears from some of the students *and* teachers!

The north-east at last... At last I'm going to the place where the Lord is sending me to work. But patience is a great

31

thing, and I'm sure that this inactive time of preparation will be repaid a hundredfold...

The Mardi Gras carnival was something fantastic – it was the greatest luck to be here and take part in two days of it, Saturday and Sunday. It really was a sight to see. There were no longer just people walking in the streets; there was a delirious crowd, wholly possessed by the rhythm of the samba. There were no mere spectators – everyone was performing. We went up the Avenida Rio Branco and the Avenida Presidente Vargas (the Champs Élysées of Rio) several times, and sometimes we could hardly push our way along. You may say that I don't believe in original sin, but I was struck by how different this was from what you see all over France, or anywhere else; not the famous sensuality we so often hear condemned, but a truly popular and poetic carnival. It is a kind of going back to the roots of things: the Brazilian people go back to their deepest origins – the Indian forests (the costumes, the cries, the songs), Africa, with its magic and ritual and its luxuriance – not to mention the great human themes of death, fate, love, poverty, suffering.

Raymond and I were visiting a Brazilian doctor in Rio, who took us to the carnival on those two days. But the Brazilians have far fewer inhibitions, far less rigidity, far less conventionality than the French. Life is simpler: the doctor is a man who spends the day at home wearing nothing but shorts – no shirt, no socks, no shoes. He dresses up and joins in the carnival just like anyone else, for these are his people, and he is one of them. We went swimming together at Copacabana, and talked of Péguy and Léon Bloy. He isn't a practising Catholic, but he is looking for the truth. Despite all his many objections to the Church he honours the true God, a God of love to whom he offers himself already in a sense – for every week, outside his regular practice, he spends a great part of his time giving free help to people in two shanty-towns. And incidentally, it was there that he met the thing that sparked off his conversion, through witnessing the life of the Little Sisters of Charles de Foucauld . . .

I enclose a few photos. Thank Brigitte for her letter. I hope you're all keeping well. Is the winter over?

Part 2
The revolution of love

DIARY

I met a woman who lives alone. Her husband has left her and gone off into the interior.

Salaries: a girl working in the town earns 2,000 cruzeiros a month (less than 5 dollars).

Another, in an office: 2,500 cruzeiros a month (about 5½ dollars).

A tram driver: he starts at five in the morning, which means leaving home at four. He works till one thirty; or, he may do a different shift, from four in the afternoon until half past midnight. He frequently does overtime; he gets the minimum official wage of 12,000 cruzeiros a month (about 26 dollars).

The rent for a wretched house in 'Brasília':* 2,500 cruzeiros a month.

A family with eleven children, and both parents working. The mother spends all day in a factory, while the children stay at home on their own. There is a girl of sixteen and one of fifteen; there are two boys without jobs.

Found one house full of *cachaça* (alcohol made from sugar cane).

Promotion means having a nice house. One man thinks the union is all right (the union of the neighbourhood community – these are groups that are growing up a lot in our neighbourhood). The union is all right, but 'I haven't time for it'. He is buying bricks to build a better house.

I am continually asked: do you like being in Piraï?

---

* This is not the capital city referred to earlier, but one of the more squalid districts of S., named after the capital in irony.

LETTER

To *his family and friends*: At last I am writing to you from
S. At the end of February, Yves and I finished our course at
Petrópolis, and a few days later we left Rio de Janeiro by air –
having been given two free tickets out of the truly Brazilian
kindness of the Cruzeiro do Sul and Pan Air.

S. is a small city of 180,000 inhabitants (some say 200,000).
It is one of the oldest and most old-fashioned in Brazil as
regards the architecture of houses and churches. It is actually
an island. The 'Sudene' (north-east development scheme) is
planning to build a harbour, but unfortunately at the
moment there is only a tiny fishing port. S. is the capital of
the most under-developed state in the whole north-east, and
the north-east is the most undeveloped part of the whole of
Brazil. This state is under-developed economically (archaic
agricultural methods, small, non-modernized industries);
culturally; politically (demagogy); and sociologically (the
property system is manifestly unjust and inefficient). The
result is poverty, despair, hunger and passivity ... Yet the
state has a future. Between some states which are continually
flooded, and others where there is always drought, the state
of S. has both fertile soil and water as well as warmth. That
is why we are witnessing a lot of internal immigration : from
the interior of the country to S., and from S. to the south. I
may add that the state of S. is like China, one of the areas of
the world in which the birth index is highest (though offset,
alas, by the highest infant mortality rate in the world). The
state has doubled its population in twelve years: from
1,583,000, it had become 2,432,000 by 1960, and is about
3,000,000 now.

The archdiocese of S. comprises over 65,000 square miles,
and 1,500,000 people. For this vast and vital work, how many
priests do you think it 'possesses'? Forty seculars and twenty-

nine regulars – a grand total of sixty-nine. With Yves and myself, seventy-one. The situation is desperate.

We received a warm welcome at the archbishop's palace – a three-hundred-year-old edifice – from the archbishop, Dom Renaldo, who is a friendly, straightforward man, and Dom Poletta, his auxiliary, who shows a bold missionary spirit. As soon as we got there, we began to visit the different parts of the city, especially the working-class areas. We were lucky in having an ACO member as our guide, Pedro, a Negro, who was born, and has always lived, among the people and who, by dint of trade union work (he has just been elected a full-time organizer of the textiles union), has gradually achieved a remarkable advance as a human being. We visited several factories: for cotton spinning and weaving, hemp spinning and weaving, and the extraction of oil from the *babaçu*, which is a kind of coconut. We went into several bars where prostitution is carried on; met some of the trade unionists; visited the homes of various ACO people, etc. Yves and I were given neighbouring parishes to look after: Yves 'João Bello' (working class, lower middle class, and some upper middle class), and myself 'Piraï'.

Now I must tell you about my parish, Piraï. I can hardly call it a parish, for only one per cent of the people come to church. Piraï is just over two miles wide, bordered by the sea. With Fr Lucio de Jesus, a Brazilian priest of twenty-seven, I went out to get to know my parish, and believe me, it is fearful: poverty, hunger, sub-human living conditions, promiscuity, no work, no money: in short the sub-proletariat, with all that that implies. The people live in huts of wood and beaten earth with roofs of palm leaves. A great many of them are built on stilts (rather like the lake cities of two thousand years ago) to escape the stagnant water of the *lama*, a kind of disgusting mud brought up periodically by the sea. At any moment it could all collapse. The whole neighbourhood is criss-crossed by appalling streams of sewage which you cross on planks or by stepping-stones. The 'high street' is simply the largest of three streams – the one which brings together all the city's refuse.

The area is alive with children, most of them naked, with swollen stomachs due to malnutrition and worms. They swarm everywhere, along with numbers of black pigs, which seem to be in their element. The *casa parroquial* – the presbytery, that is – is just another hut, perhaps slightly less awful, but just like the rest: tiny, fragile, made of wood and at the mercy of all the winds of heaven. Lucio built it himself with the help of volunteers. That is where I am to live, and my hammock is ready for me (everyone here sleeps in hammocks). When I first arrived, Lucio had just borrowed some money from neighbours, for he was short of cash. He wants to live as a poor man among the poor and, please God, I intend to do the same.

Our church is a simple wooden hut, beautiful in its poverty. A few benches, a table for mass which is said every day facing the people. Next Sunday I shall be officially introduced to 'my people' there, after a day of recollection with the Catholic lay groups during which Yves and I can get to know the leaders. Yves (together with Lucio) will take charge of the local YCW and I shall have the two adult workers' groups launched recently with the help of Dom Poletta, but functioning without a chaplain, and also a group of beginners. Later, who knows? ... other things may develop.

The first task of our community of priests and laymen in Piraï is not to fill our church or get people to the sacraments, but to create, or help to form, natural communities among them. How can you preach about what the gospel teaches, or about heaven and hell, to people living in sub-human conditions? What right have we to try to stick the supernatural on top of a nature that is almost non-existent? But human solidarity, giving oneself to others in the common struggle against poverty and despair, these are the beginnings of a road towards the Lord, indeed a sign that the Lord is there, already at work in men's hearts, and calling them nearer day by day, that he is already at work in the heart of this human community, gradually transforming it into his kingdom. What matters is not to fill the churches, but for the kingdom of God to come, and it will come through love: *Ubi caritas et amor Deus ibi est*, 'Where charity and love are, God is.' Wherever men forget their own self-interest to form a community, they are on the way to God. God is there, already, among them, creating his kingdom... 'Many of those who are God's are not the Church's, and many who are the Church's are not God's,' said St Augustine.

To conclude – here are a few figures. Do you know what a working man earns here? The minimum wage laid down by law is 400 cruzeiros a day (which is well under a dollar), but the employer keeps eight per cent for social security (he is supposed to pay another eight per cent himself, but all too often he simply pockets the lot); so the worker has 368 cruzeiros a day as his sole income, on which to keep his wife and children (often numerous). 'It's a miracle that they survive,' said Pedro. Meat is 300–400 cruzeiros a kilo, rice 120–130. And I may add that the minimum wage is always the maximum! Even a highly qualified worker is unlikely to earn more. At the most he will get a supplement of up to 4,000 cruzeiros a month (rather less than 9 dollars), if the employer so pleases. Anyway, a great proportion of wage-earners don't even get the minimum. A lot of women in the spinning factory are paid piece-work rates, and to earn more than, at most, 7,000 cruzeiros a month (a little over 15 dollars) would be a miracle.

Even to be in regular work is a privilege – those who are are the exception in Piraï. If I think back to poor people I knew in France I realize that here they would be rich, very rich indeed.

Pray for me, dear friends, that I may respond generously, and above all, joyfully, to the Lord's call. Pray for Brazil, for the state of S. where there is such destitution, and where we should be fighting poverty from all sides at once, but where, none the less, there is such wealth too – a wealth of love almost ready to set off a mighty explosion. When it finally does so, a whole rotten world of selfishness will be destroyed. Wealth untapped, wealth as yet unexploited ... the field of the Lord is vast.

If you come to visit me here, you will find a sentence from Mauriac written in Portuguese above the door : 'The moment your heart stops burning with love, those beside you will die of cold.'

May the fire of the Lord dwell in us all, bringing light, purification and joy.

S. Piraï
27 March 1963

LETTER

To his parents: I am living the most difficult, but also the most wonderful days of my life... Yesterday, as I went to bed, I was thinking that I am a bit like Job; and seeing from my hammock a lizard crawling along the wall, I said to the Lord : 'The Lord gave, and the Lord has taken away; blessed be the name of the Lord !' I've preached it often enough; now I can keep quiet and live it !

For the past week I have been visiting people in their huts from morning to night. Wonderful work, but the poverty is incredible. That is why the Lord wanted me to be poor too, so I can go into the houses of poor people, so I can sit with them on their rickety stools...

I sometimes envy the children who speak Portuguese so effortlessly, while I still have such trouble with it, but it is better this way; when I go into a house I think of myself as a child, I don't know what to say, but feel so content, and the

Lord helps me so much, that I can communicate just the same.

We have a marvellous community here, united in spirit and one in our determination to live poor among the poor. The house is always open, and there is a continual coming and going, especially of young people. Everything belongs to all, and everything is free in the parish – no mass stipends!

Lucio is a terrific priest, and we work together wonderfully well. As well as the parish, he is specially concerned with the boys and girls in the YCW. It is strange how identical are our ways of thinking and our approach to the lay apostolate. But he reminds me of la Minotière, with his endless meetings; even he realizes that he must cut down on them a bit. We can work it out together. But don't think of us as a community of two, for we are six. There are Joaquim and Flavio, two YCW members who work in the city and come back here in the evenings (Joaquim is an area leader); there is Jose Fernandez and there is Pedro, who also works in the city and comes back in the evening. Our life is an original and unusual experience: a team of priests and laymen who discuss our life together, share our money, and pray together...

What can I tell you about the parish? I have already seen and heard so much... In one street I visited there are eight or ten women and girls who are prostitutes – eight or ten known ones, that is to say, not to mention the others. But poverty is a vicious circle in which they are all entrapped: no work, no money, no food, no home, no human life, no education, no health, and so it goes on... Who would cast the first stone and preach morality to them? I am sure these women are with the Lord, even when they're with their customers. Again and again, I have seen evidence of generosity among them, a readiness for self-sacrifice, for love. I often think of that memorable saying of Christ's: 'The harlots go into the kingdom of God before you.'

There is so much to tell... When I get back from visiting I

43

note down the things that have most struck me. I can still, for instance, feel burning into me the look of total wretchedness of a mother of four, with a fifth on the way, who lives in an appalling hut with two dark rooms (and a high rent). Two beautiful eyes filled with resignation and despair. At such times as this, words are pointless, and my poverty is transformed into wealth, the wealth of God and his love. When I asked her where she put her children to sleep, she showed me one pathetic bed – and there, higgledy-piggledy, six people sleep, and it will soon be seven.

Another horrible sight (though I see things like it daily) was that of three children crawling about on the beaten earth, round a repulsive plate, and fighting like dogs over a few mouthfuls of rice mixed with cassava-flour * – the only food they have here.

When I think of what gets thrown into our dustbins...

The children already know me. When I go along what they call a street, they rush up, some wearing pants, some wearing nothing at all, and shout, 'Padre Paolo, Padre Paolo, benção' (Father Paul, bless me...).

Well, I've talked about nothing but myself. How is everything at home? ... I've had no letters for some time. The mail is undoubtedly very irregular here. I enclose a few snaps. I'll leave you for now – my greetings to everyone.

March 1963

DIARY

A mother's reaction to her daughter's illness : 'God helps me, I trust him. I've never destroyed a child in my womb, like some people. We must respect life. It comes from God. I'm sure God will take account of that.'

* Because it is cheap, the flour obtained from the tropical root cassava (or manioc) forms a substantial element in the diet of the Brazilian poor. Unfortunately it has practically no food value.

Many couples haven't been married in church.

There are pictures of nudes on a lot of walls next to pictures of the saints.

The reaction of one person with a sick child in the house: 'Father, have you no medicine?'

We must make people want a neighbourhood union to improve this situation – to build a dispensary and get hold of a doctor...

Syphilis: one young man is paralysed by it. They tell me it comes from the father, it comes from the parents (that's what his mother says). It comes from the ancestors – who are laughing about it now.

A lot of girls go to work in Rio ... the problem of the big cities.

A mother advises her son to leave the state of S. She says, 'There's no future here.'

A great many families include nephews, grandchildren, cousins... Evidently the Brazilian family is open, not closed. The reverse is true in most of the most advanced countries.

The theme: *Brasil é um colosso* (Brazil is a colossus). One constantly hears it; it's a colossus in wealth and splendour, but at the same time, for various reasons, it is under-developed: because of the political situation, some say, from lack of technologists, because of illiteracy – there are plenty of reasons to put forward.

S. Piraï
Sunday 7 April 1963

LETTER

To his parents: Yes, Father, you're quite right to remind me what a myth it is to talk of ever being 'settled'. The Lord has taken me at my word, and now he is leading me by the hand along the roads of suffering and happiness.

People dying of hunger... Even reading about it is a bit upsetting, but when you are actually sitting in their homes, when you can talk to them, when you see just what they do eat, when you have baptized six newly-born babies at home in five days because they are in danger of dying, and so on endlessly, then you can't sleep in peace ever again... A priest always eventually becomes the father of a huge family – his parish. It's anguishing, but it's a joy as well. It seems to me that being a father is the finest thing in the world. I walk through my neighbourhood, saying hello on all sides, letting all the children push me around and spending some time with them. I walk and walk, and the next day I go out again, and it's really no different from la Minotière or la Bastelle. I am the father, I'm the person who brings the Father to them. They have a Father in heaven, and aren't just left to sink or swim in their poverty. There's a gleam of light in their darkness, a bit of blue sky to defeat despair.

In the evenings I come home with a heart full to bursting, yet also feeling something of God's own love for them. We are lucky enough to have mass every evening at six. I'm not keen on thinking of God as 'good' – I'd rather think of him as loving and kind.

22 April 1963

LETTER

To his parents: There is always plenty to do here, and our home is a goldfish bowl which makes it hard to get the peace and quiet you need in order to think. For instance I'm finding it incredibly hard to get this letter written.

I'm still doing a lot of house-to-house visiting, and I don't know whether I'll ever get round the whole area, for it's enormous. Quite fascinating. There's nothing like personal contact to get to know what a place is really like. These encounters *are* the Church, as far as I'm concerned: Christ working within people and helping them to see light beyond their sufferings, to find a meaning in life, a real hope, and also helping them to begin to work up a revolutionary ferment – for though Christ loved poverty, he can't accept this kind of total destitution. He wants us all to help in bringing about the revolution of love.

At the moment I am alone here, and have been for three weeks, because Lucio is away preaching two retreats. It's a useful apprenticeship for me.

Holy Week was wonderful – not, of course, in the traditional style, but in our own missionary style. We worked out a kind of para-liturgy to show that the mass is a family meal, and that Jesus came to prove to us that God is a Father and we his children, a Father who proves his love for his children by giving his life for them: this bread he gives them to eat is his own body and blood. And out here, how true that is ... (all this, of course, was on Maundy Thursday). A member of the Catholic university students' organization (YCS) came to help us with Holy Week. Brazilian young people have a real hunger for truth, a real thirst for the gospel.

The Easter vigil was terrific. We did the whole thing out of doors. I incensed the paschal candle with a censer we had made ourselves, a Nescafé tin hung on an iron chain – far handsomer than all those complicated gold ones they have in cathedrals. At the offertory everyone brought some food: rice, fish, cassava cakes. And after mass we communicated under the stars, sharing this poor man's food. The Church of the poor is truly beautiful.

I seldom wear a cassock, just a sports shirt and trousers. I've cut the sleeves off all my shirts and stitched a cross over the heart. That's the easiest costume. It certainly doesn't worry anyone here, and probably in a few years they'll be doing it everywhere. You should see the children running to meet me: 'Padre Paolo!' Children and the childlike in heart don't need a cassock to recognize a priest. . .

Every Sunday, from six in the evening until dawn, a group, the 'Bom-ba-Meu-Boi', play outside our hut, and the hypnotic rhythm acts as a lullaby. All of African folklore is expressed in these dances, and they suddenly take one right back to their origins. The rhythm literally takes possession of me. We listen and listen. The melody always begins with an improvisation on a simple theme by one leader (rather like a Negro spiritual); then everyone takes it up, the whole orchestra, and they amplify it and bring it alive; it reaches a climax, and then the leader whistles, and they stop and start again with another melodic phrase. We want to adapt Christian themes: yesterday evening we worked out a few themes in this way to fit each melody. The Church is catholic, which means that she must want each one of her peoples to keep its own culture. This will enrich the rest of the family, especially when it is a culture that really expresses the soul of the people concerned. When that soul is expressed, it is always in relation to the drama of life; and how can the Church respond to the people if she does not get close to their forms of expression?

Well, I must stop for today. Please forgive me for not writing oftener or more regularly.

DIARY

There are lots of little schools: a woman or girl who can barely read and write will teach thirty or more children aged five to six. And there are classes for older ones until seven in the evening.

I've seen pictures on walls of St Joan of Arc, Our Lady of Fatima, St George, St Joseph.

In one house there is a large altar to St Joseph.

The Adventists (a Christian sect) are going from house to house.

The case of Antonio: he goes to the Protestant church on Sunday morning, and to the Catholic church in the afternoon.

Two boys aged thirteen and fifteen, and they couldn't find Brazil on the map.

Most of the families in this district come from the interior. There are continual removals, people coming and going in the neighbourhood. Some have come since I got here, from other Brazilian states near and far.

A characteristic remark, in a house where three women live: 'There are no men here, only children.' The three women each have two or three children. The house has three rooms.

A general impression: the people and the dogs all seem dead. You see it in their eyes and the way they stand. The eyes will often speak when the mouth is saying nothing. You can read a lot in eyes: for instance, total despair and at the same time a certain magnificent resignation – but this is something no Christian can accept.

S., 18 May 1963

LETTER

To *his parents*: Life in Piraï goes on – with apostolic work, joy, and hot weather. In this climate you certainly know you are alive; and more important than the weather is the atmosphere of our hut, with its sense of fellowship and the great joy we have.

Padre... The overtones of this word are something almost unknown in France – it has a quite unique human warmth. Georges, a Canadian, interpreter and assistant to the director of the centre in Petrópolis, came to see us and was astounded by it. 'I've been to a lot of lectures,' he said as we went through the streets of our neighbourhood, 'but I've never seen anything like this ... a Church really established right in among the poor, really in touch with them. A really missionary ministry in action, working from natural base communities.'

Yesterday was the anniversary of Lucio's ordination. We arranged a little party: mass, and then talk, singing, accordion, games. We ended up with a real orgy of singing, with a pure Brazilian beat to it, and everyone going quite mad. I danced like a lunatic. It was great.

It was the fourth or fifth time the people have had a party with us, like that, outdoors: it makes us feel we are real neighbours. What else can we do together? I am obsessed with the importance of creating base communities.

Lucio's work is mainly centred on 'Brasília', one of the sections of Piraï where the people are the poorest of all (the name was chosen as a joke at the time when they were building the ultra-modern capital of Brazil). The whole place is built *on mud*, and at high tide all the houses have the sea coming in, even though they stand on stilts. Living conditions are unspeakable, hygiene non-existent. You would have to see it for yourselves to realize what it's like. You'd have to see inside the huts, having crossed the mud by balancing precariously on planks six or ten feet above ground; you'd have to see where they sleep, where the women do the cooking and sit all day, what they eat, and what a state their children are in.

Led by a former YCW member, and inspired by their own desperate need, a little base community is gradually forming: twelve women or girls of the neighbourhood who can sew and embroider, etc. (they have some kind of certificate) have agreed to teach the others; so there are now twelve 'classes' for 130 girls (sewing, binding, cutting, handicrafts, knitting). Not only are these 130 girls escaping from despair and idleness by learning a trade, but they will also be able to bring a bit of money home by forming a selling 'cooperative'. The classes take place in the poor shaky huts of 'Brasília', but since they are really getting to be too small, the people have decided to buy some ground and build a bigger hut.

Yesterday I went with the boys and girls from 'Brasília' on a picnic they had organized by the sea (we all packed into an uncovered truck). Then, after mass, sixty or seventy of us, led by Lucio, were to go to meet the owner of the ground on which we were to build the said hut. Twenty-two of the young men were to collect enough stones, between ten in the evening and three in the morning, to cover the ground, hoping to start building the next night. But then someone suggested another bit of ground farther away, because it would be easier.

We are all four ready to die of hunger, or perhaps of love, for the revolution of love must certainly begin here one day. Indeed, I think it's already beginning here in Piraï.

DIARY

A lot of men work as masons.

Hygiene, health, food : I've seen a lot of lunches and dinners being made. I've never seen any salad, any fruit, any green vegetables : therefore I've never seen any vitamins. Yesterday I saw fifteen or twenty tins of food which the women were using to make dinner for the workers in the Matadoro factory. The food looked dirty – more suitable to feed to animals. I have even heard someone say, 'We fill our stomachs, but we aren't eating.'

In France I've seen dogs eat better and cleaner food.

You do see little islands of cleanliness amid all the filth. One young woman is clean and even quite smart. Her house is well arranged and actually has a certain human dignity about it – yet it's built just the same as all the others, out of earth, wood and straw. But her husband is a mason; and she, one can see, has had a bit of education.

This morning I saw a dog fight. It was ghastly ... a fight for life. 'Fight' is a word you often hear here.

LETTER

To his former parishioners and friends: I'm taking advantage
of a torrential downpour this morning to send you some news
(it is the rainy season from now till well into June). By now
I'm well established in my district of Piraï. I 'settled in' (! !)
two months ago, and am part of a parish community with
Padre Lucio, Joaquim and Jose Fernandez; the greater part of
my time is spent visiting people. These visits, these basic contacts, are very important, not simply in order to get right
inside the reality of Brazil, but, with my priest's heart and
my mind, to get right inside the reality of destitution. There
are some things that can't be put into words – they can only
be 'felt' – and a priest must get to suffer *inside* his people's
suffering, and hope *inside* their hope; it can't be achieved in a
day. But one must also consider what can be done about this
utter poverty, physical and spiritual both. This is where a
team of priests and laymen like ours is such an advantage:
we have not only a wealth of brotherly affection, but the
whole wealth of the Church and her mission. We are looking
for the answers together. We want to build the Church here,
and it will of necessity be the Church of the poor. That is
why we cannot live other than as poor among the poor. We
can clearly see that human salvation goes hand in hand with
'Christian' salvation. . .

The only thing here is to get people into communities, to
help them out of their individualism (the fierce struggle for
life – that is, literally the fight not to die . . .). Our common
enemy number one is paternalism, because it's the wrong
answer; it can never destroy poverty, and in any case it goes
against God's plan. God wants to save his people not from
outside themselves, but starting from the talents and gifts he
has given them. . . You can't escape from poverty without
being first aware that it *is* poverty, nor without realizing the
talents the Lord has placed in us, even the least among us.

You can't 'escape' spiritually into Christ without at the same time forming 'a people', the people of God – not artificially held together by a vague set of beliefs, but brought together naturally in love. Our work, both priests and laymen, is therefore to start from life itself to build up and strengthen base communities, to give them self-awareness by a certain minimum of education in human living (starting always from the necessities of life, and leaving 'organization' till later; giving them a sense of community and getting them to share responsibilities), and gradually leading them to Christ: I've never before understood as I do here that *the Church* is the Church of the poor, and that the Church is 'the people of God advancing'. I feel that I am at the moment going through an exceptional phase of my life as a priest. The Lord be praised, for it's a great grace. If it weren't pride, I'd even say, 'My voices have not deceived me' in sending me here, to follow the Pope's call. And I'm so wonderfully happy... I couldn't hide the fact if I wanted to. I think the main reason for it is the poverty we are trying to live. When you have nothing, you feel light, you feel at the disposition of everyone and everything, you feel *free*! When I got here two months ago, Lucio showed me my room – it was empty, not even a hammock in it. We borrowed one, and later some of my new parishioners clubbed together to buy one for me. Even harder perhaps than this material poverty is the interior poverty of abandoning one's cultural roots as a European so as to gradually form a new, Brazilian self... In France I ate rice once a year; here, I have it twice a day. In France, I never had an afternoon rest; here I rest for at least an hour (we have to, because of the heat, and also because we get so little sleep at night – going to bed often after midnight and getting up between five thirty and six for the first mass at six). I often spend two or three weeks without speaking a word of French (I only speak it when I'm alone with Yves, and occasionally with Lucio). Yet I've not felt any special sense of exile –

hardly more than when I left the miners' tenements of la Minotière behind for the unaccustomed sound of cows mooing at la Bastelle.

What else can I tell you? That Lucio and I get on like two brothers, of one mind and one pastoral spirit. That our order of priorities starts with the forming of base communities, and then the problem of the children's classes which we are in the middle of reorganizing in little groups of eight or ten, with someone in charge of each group, which meets in their home. It's difficult, and most necessary. What is hard is to secure continuing support and enthusiasm from the catechists (there's a week's catechetical course going on at the moment). Lucio gives a great deal of time and most of his evenings to the YCW, boys and girls both. (He is almost the only chaplain in S.!) I myself am chaplain to the local ACO (which will soon break up into two groups), and am expecting to take over the two other groups in S. as well... Dom Poletta was really the only other chaplain except Lucio for all the Christian worker groups in S. – which tells you how badly my help was needed here. The training of active laymen is not merely required by the demands of the Church, but is an absolute necessity for Brazil and all of Latin America. There are two reasons: first, a sentimental and superstitious piety can't stand up for long against the movement of history, and second, everyone in Brazil is convinced that revolution is bound to come. And who will make a revolution of love if it isn't Christians who have received the revelation of love?

It seems to me that in these days, especially since the Council, the Lord wants us to be bolder and bolder. We have grown all too used to seeing people living in poverty, too accustomed to compromising between the demands of the gospel and the power of money, too accustomed to labelling everyone 'communist' who makes any attack on the established *disorder*, too accustomed to the easy way out, to reducing religion to no more than church-going; and so on, and so on. What do you think? Could it be that Christ, at this very moment, is inviting each one of us to a new display of daring – daring in faith (getting out of our old habits of thought: actually thinking our faith, translating our faith into the tragic and marvellous reality of the present time) – daring in hope (the Lord is in the process of saving our generation... He has sown fruitful seed in the hearts of the men of our time, which we must exploit, which we must reveal to them) – daring in charity, in love: it is love that has saved and will save us all. Love can make revolutions. The revolution the Third World needs is a revolution of love, of the love that can make revolutions.

In conclusion, I should like to leave you with a thought I've been mulling over for the past few days: 'There are many ways of loving our neighbour, but there is only one way of loving God – and that is loving our neighbour.'

Pray for me, pray for us all.

8 June 1963

LETTER

To his family: I'm afraid I'm not writing so often at the moment, but please don't hold it against me: 'No news is good news.' You can imagine how my life is – divided, parcelled out, not much peace for writing, since the 'open plan' of our house hardly lends itself to that; all I can do is escape from time to time, as I'm doing now. I'm writing from the seminary: in fact I have to do some work for a meeting to-morrow, a study day for the ACO group, and I must also prepare a series of sermon outlines for the clergy meeting next Wednesday, with two bishops present.

Thank you, Father, for all the news of the family – don't think I have forgotten anyone; separation makes affection purer and more intense.

Today marks the end of my first three months in S., and

55

eight months in Brazil. It is terrible how time flies. I still have the same feeling about my life here : that it is both hard and wonderful (just like the hand of God himself). Did I tell you that Lucio is staying here after all, and not going to Europe as planned? I'm delighted for the sake of our team 'experiment'. I am still getting more and more involved in the neighbourhood.

I am spending more time with the ACO; there are three groups now, and two more soon to be formed. I see Yves from time to time, which is good for us both : we can compare impressions and experiences.

S. still has no archbishop, just as the world has no pope. What a loss John XXIII will be ! ... It's only because of him, thanks to him, that I'm here.

Do you realize what an ecumenical atmosphere I'm living in? One day I stopped beside a travelling library run by the Baptists. We chatted. I invited a young pastor to visit here, and last Saturday five young Baptist pastors came to see us. It was great... We ended our meeting with each praying in his own way (for a long time now we have sung two beautiful Protestant hymns at mass – 'O Caminiu E Jesu' (The road to Heaven is Jesus), and 'Alleluia').

This is the kind of thing they say here : 'Here in Piraï it is normal and natural to be born and to die, it is the rule; the exception is to live.'

I must stop, because I have a lot of other letters to write. All goes well. Life is fine. All my love to you.

DIARY

Today I began calling in August 24th Street. Masses of children. The gutter runs down the middle of the street. When it gets filled with sea water, the children wallow in it. A lot of houses have mud and 'gardens' inside.

A woman all alone, with three children; she comes from

Rio. Her husband has left her and is looking for work. Her mother has asthma.

A man who works in the St Isabelle factory has lost heart and no longer has any faith in the trade union.

Two women making hammocks in their home.

I heard again what was mentioned at the ACO meeting the other day: the boss said he would agree not to close the factory for repairing machines, on condition that the workers started work at four in the morning.

S., 8 July 1963

LETTER

To his parents: Yesterday was a day to remember; when I came back from Ponte São Silvio (it's across the sea, and you go in a filthy little boat) where I'd been saying mass, preaching and baptizing, the parish community in Piraï gave me an unaccustomed welcome. It was the delayed celebration of my fourteenth anniversary – what an old priest I am ! There were speeches, accordion-playing (the piano of the poor), more speeches; Christian workers, young and adult, the social worker, the parish community, and Lucio; there were presents (I got a cake and some trousers), and then after a speech by Padre Paolo (the Church of the poor, but I am a poor man too like you, I have nothing to give and that is why I can give you God), the 'Bom-ba-Meu Boi' group turned up dressed in their best, to do a couple of hours' dancing in my honour. They were wearing their special festival clothes : on their heads and feet and wrists they had huge bunches of feathers; their whole bodies sparkled with colour and 'diamonds'. In the middle of the dancing there came three magnificent bulls, black as velvet, decked out in bright multicoloured streamers, red, green and blue. A splendid sight.

In the midst of it all, Dom Poletta arrived wanting me to go to the airport with him to meet a Belgian couple from Malines, who have come to Latin America on behalf of a lay missionary organization. They're very nice and have come to see the rural cooperative experiment in Marianopolis. They have promised me to call and see you one of these days.

And how is Brigitte, is she dead? You say nothing about her... Monique, how is the missions group going? Do you remember the doctors who offered me an assistant? I could do with them now! Hundreds of mothers see their children die because they haven't the money to buy medicine. The other day I snatched up a prescription and went to talk to the pharmacist; you can't just let a child die. He gave me a present of two of the necessary injection ampoules and I bought the other six. I spoke to the leader of the mothers' club; we *must* open a medical centre where people can be seen for nothing. I'll send you a list of the things we need most, and I'll write more about this later. You might begin to sound out the ground, but see whether the Catholic Assistance can do the sending because the Customs are a problem otherwise. Thank you in advance.

S., 25 July 1963

LETTER

To his parents: Well, I got back last week from Recife where the regional congress of ACO leaders took place. It was a most useful journey. I met a lot of people, and know a lot more about the north-east in general, and the world of the poor in particular; I met members of active lay groups, priests, and even bishops. I've learnt a lot; the few days in Recife, João Pessoa, Natal, and Fortaleza have particularly taught me how I can improve my work as chaplain to these groups. Everywhere I was received with open arms. I've come back determined to try to extend my ACO work in the town, and to give more time to strengthening the existing groups and to making the movement grow (there are many possibilities). I have no time to write more. All goes well. Brazil is boiling over... There could be a *coup d'état* at any minute –

from either the extreme right or the extreme left. The Communist party has made the first bid for the student world and the army; for the time being, at any rate, they have given up on the working class. That will be move two – at least that's what they say here. There is an obsessive anti-Communism here, even in the Church; as yet the privileged class will not open their eyes to what's going on. The way of Christians may be hard, but at least the direction is plain to see.

30 July 1963

LETTER

To *his parents*: After a most interesting study week with the priests of the archdiocese, I have just taken part in another study week near S. with the YCW. It was a regional congress of forty or so active members of both sexes from our state and the next. We were four chaplains, with Lucio, Yves and myself. It was an exciting week. Each evening I came back to say mass in Piraï, but often went back for the rest of the night. During one late night conversation, I talked about my impressions and memories of being a YCW chaplain in France. Dom Poletta was there for half of the time.

At the end of that week, I had the luck to take part in a *romaria*, a typically Brazilian kind of pilgrimage, very colourful, and concluding with a 'promise'. A great many people here make promises to the saints. I was actually invited by the Santa Clara factory who were making the pilgrimage, because the workers knew me as chaplain to the ACO and priest of a working-class parish. (The whole thing goes back three or four years, to when there was a threat to close down these textile factories; at the time they made a promise that they would go on pilgrimage to S.R. every year if their factory did not close). We did about twenty miles on foot – from S. to S.R. – it took from ten in the evening till four thirty in the morning. It was a fantastic journey, quite indescribable.

The whole group prayed; fine; then they sang religious hymns; and finally, they sang sambas, tangos and *baions*. We had a little *cachaça* (sugar-cane liquor) but not too much. Whenever we stopped, everyone would open their bags and have a little bread with dried fish, or some cassava flour, or a cassava cake, or some 'cola-jesus' to drink. I gave an extempore talk on what saints are – what they are doing up there, why we pray to them, how they can sometimes do miracles. Suddenly a man broke in : *'Eu peco a palavra'* which means, 'I want to say something'. And he said to the others, 'Is it right for us to listen to the Padre with our hats on?' – looking pointedly at one of his mates, who agreed and took off his hat! But two minutes later the hatless one asked to speak. Silence all round. 'Is it right to listen to the Padre without a shirt on?' – and he looked at the first man. Everyone laughed, and the first accuser was forced to put on his shirt. I got back to my theme without any trouble.

When we got to S.R., everyone lay down to sleep on the ground round the church, waiting for it to be opened. A few went to swim in the sea nearby. I said mass and preached, thinking of my duty to evangelize on the basis of reality as I found it – a reality very different from anything we know in France. But I've already almost forgotten France... So much wealth, so many talents are left untapped here.

That sense of unity I got on our twenty-mile walk, during which I felt engulfed by these people, and yet accepted like a brother, proves what a great capacity they have for welcoming, what a longing for the supernatural; it seems to me that the African rhythms, popular music, dancing and the long sad songs you hear in the night are all so much evidence of that longing...

I'm going to be alone for the next month or so. Lucio is going for a holiday to his family, business-people near Barnaiba.

I'm still busy visiting. I often bring home masses of

bananas, oranges, coconuts, eggs, sugar-cane; sometimes even writing paper...

There's a lot more to say, but I haven't time, so I send you my love.

DIARY

Health and the doctor: there is a woman with pains in her stomach, and no money to go to the doctor; and no doctor will agree to come into the neighbourhood.

Today I saw a paralysed little girl of fourteen, looking like a skeleton. But they accept poverty fatalistically.

An excellent response for the Uniao dos Moradores (union of neighbourhood communities): 'We should get together to make things better in the street.' When anything of this sort begins I'm ready to do whatever I can.

One old man wept as he talked to me: he is paralysed, but he can't go to hospital because he has no money.

Many of the women – most, perhaps – have no husbands.

One man: five children; he's a docker and has had to stop work. His wife works too. He drinks. Life in their home is one long quarrel; the other day he stole a crate of sardines and was caught. The whole family clubbed together to pay, so that he wouldn't go to prison and no one would find out.

A worker in the spinning factory: this month he didn't get the minimum salary. He is paid piece-work rates, and in eight days he only earned what he normally earns in one, because his machine was idle from lack of cotton to work on.

A man from the interior killed someone in his own village; he then came to S. with his wife and children, but now he's sleeping with his sister-in-law too. She already has two grandchildren. They occupy a different room, so now he has two wives to keep – two homes, two families.

In the soap factory, two workers were made to do the work of three. They went to see the boss; not merely would he not

61

hear what they had to say, but he suspended them both for a fortnight. Fifteen other workers went to the director to complain, and the boss then suspended them for ten days too, claiming that they had gone away on another job. There was no organized union there at the time, but since then they have begun to form one.

Rua do Posso (Well Street): in one house the privy, a very crude one too, is about five feet from the kitchen. There are eight children, all ill.

Food for thought: 'When there's money we eat rice and cassava flour; when there isn't any, just coffee with cassava flour.' There are seven children in that family.

One mother with eight kids, and her husband gone. She works at the factory, spinning.

Two women from the interior ask me, 'Why are some people rich and some poor? Why are some people sick and some healthy? We've just got to put up with it.' 'I know the story of Job,' said one, 'and it's the same for us, don't you think, Father?'

My reply: 'Yes it's true, there *are* some things you've just got to put up with, but there are some things we can't tolerate. Real grinding poverty, hunger, filthy houses, and such. We can't tolerate all this because it's against God's plan which is a plan of love. We must fight it, all together. Here in Well Street, for instance.'

In the past five days I've baptized six babies in danger of death in their homes. The infant mortality is appalling.

In the state of S. the most *optimistic* figures give those out of work as seventy-five per cent of the population.

In a street in the Matadouro section, I met some Adventists. We talked about the Bible, our Lady, the superstitiousness of so many Catholics, the cult of images, the coming return of the Lord which Catholics don't seem to expect or hope for. The main problem is one of education, of forming Christians.

A quite young girl; she was taking some kind of medicine to 'get rid' of her child, to kill the child in her womb; but the child was born, so she killed it then, and made a hole in the kitchen floor and buried it. She said afterwards, 'I was afraid I wouldn't be able to bring him up, I haven't any money, I'm too poor to bring up a child.'

Case reported by a Catholic Action worker:

A family who had been living with just the vital minimum they needed, suddenly had some bad luck and were in great want. There is nothing in the house: they've lost everything. But they have responded marvellously. They are struggling, but don't want to show how poor they are. This worker went to visit them, but as a Christian should, doing all she could to prevent their feeling ashamed.

Another case:

In a spinning factory in S. a worker was at a machine. His cotton ran out, and he turned to his neighbour, a friend whose machine had plenty still, and who lent him some. The foreman was furious, and on the spot he suspended the friend who had helped him, for several days. The first man was so angry and upset that he didn't go to work either, so as to make common cause with his mate.

Fortaleza
17 September 1963

LETTER

To his family: Recife, João Pessoa, Escada, Paulista, Natal, Fortaleza – I'm at the end of a marvellous journey through the north-east.

Many new and wonderful discoveries. At Recife there was an excellent regional meeting of the ACO. I spent several days there in order to make contact with various other lay movements.

I visited a working-class district rather like Piraï, sub-proletarian, but slightly less desperately poor (all things are

63

relative), where a Belgian priest is working. I took part in several ACO meetings in the city and in the suburbs.

Recife is in a ferment, as is the whole north-east at the moment. There's a textile-workers' strike, a bank strike, and others. I visited various trade unions, and went to a meeting of the textile strikers. At Recife there is a great awareness of what the working class can achieve. The city is also expanding fast economically, as is Fortaleza. Recife is the third largest city in Brazil, with three million inhabitants, only a little smaller than São Paulo and Rio. Fortaleza is nearing a million.

At Escada we had a small impromptu meeting with the strikers to discuss the strike (I was applauded by the strikers). We visited the Archbishop of Recife, and I also had the pleasure of visiting the young French couple, Gerard and Antoinette, who were on the boat with me last year. (It is just a year ago today, 17 September, that I embarked at Marseilles.) From Recife I went by coach to João Pessoa with Pedro: we were invited there by the ACO leaders. There too we visited the unions, the families of some Christian workers, went to ACO meetings, called on the bishop, went to the beach and swam, etc. We stayed wth Dom Poletta's brother, an ACO leader... I'm repaying Dom Poletta's kindness in going to see you in France, by visiting his father and mother Who live in João Pessoa. From there we came back to Recife, where I got a plane for Natal, while Pedro went back to S. to return to his full-time work for the textile union.

At Natal I stayed with a wonderful young couple, both ACO leaders; they are the new Catholic Church, young and dynamic, which is gradually bursting out of the old framework, by dint of patience, suffering and hope. There in Natal, too, they had a whole programme lined up for me, with hardly an hour free – visits to working-class neighbourhoods, meetings with priests and with the auxiliary bishop, Dom Alfonso (the archbishop himself is old and blind), a visit to a printing works, to the Federation of Rural Trades Unions, to the Movement for Basic Education (MEB),* to two ACO groups, and last, but not least, most interesting meetings with white-collar Catholic Action groups.

The city was in a great state of upheaval, with a police strike. They have had to re-think life on strike. One of the Catholic Action leaders is a police sergeant, but that does not prevent his belonging to the working class. Just think: he earns 7,000 cruzeiros a month (which is now less than 12 dollars), plus an allowance of 2,000 (just over 3 dollars) from the Governo Estadual (the state authorities). The situation in Brazil, and in the north-east especially, could be explosive. We talked till midnight, and at three in the morning I took the coach to Fortaleza – though I had an air ticket, I wanted to see the *sertao* at close quarters. Natal to Fortaleza is fifteen hours by coach (though scarcely more than an hour by plane), along an unbelievable made-up road with enormous potholes, which looks like the worst kind of country lane in the most backward part of France.

I made the trip with an ACO leader from Fortaleza, formerly a YCW member, Maria-Regina. When we got to Fortaleza there was a mass, supper at the house of Catarina, another ACO leader, and then an informal evening with the ACO. Yesterday I visited Radio Assunçao (the radio station of the archdiocese), chatted with various trade union leaders, visited the headquarters of the banking and seamen's unions,

* This is a private organization in Brazil. Founded and run by laymen, and supported by the bishops, its object is to provide the proletariat and sub-proletariat of the country with the rudiments of education: enough to enable them to begin to develop humanly and economically. This is done through radio programmes; courses are being arranged in hygiene and business training, and so on. But all the time, alongside these methods, the movement is trying to impart a deeper spirit: to persuade people that the inhuman situation they are living in can and must be transformed, and that it is they themselves who, if they work together, will transform it.

65

as well as a very old-fashioned bottle factory, the university, the MEB, a working-class district, etc. In the evening I gave a lecture to the members of the workers' circle, which is a kind of training course for workers to help them be more active in their unions. This evening there's to be an ACO meeting in a neighbouring district. Tomorrow another district to visit, and then a meeting with the priests involved in workers' movements. Contacts with the white-collar Catholic Action groups, and with a Catholic Action body made up of young agricultural workers, students, young white-collar workers, working-class and university young people, and the evening will end with the coordinating group of the ACO.

It's funny, but true, that the arrival of Padre Paolo in Fortaleza was announced on the radio! Only in Brazil could it happen...

When Dom Renaldo found that I was spending several days in Fortaleza where he has just arrived as archbishop, he insisted that I stay at his *palacio*, and that's where I am writing from. Dom Renaldo, who used to be our bishop in S., welcomed me with open arms. He's a fine man and he cares nothing for protocol, so we can be quite relaxed with him. I march through the reception rooms and sit at the bishop's table among all the monsignori and the smart cassocks, in my short-sleeved shirt. I don't even think twice about it. We *must* get rid of all this theatrical display from the past; we must live with the living and let the rest die.

This trip has been a tremendous experience. The day after tomorrow, I shall get on a plane for the last time, to go back to S. I'll be glad to be back in my Piraï, my community, glad and ready to get back to work.

... I'm afraid I have talked only of myself, I just hope it all interests you. Anyway, cheers for Brazil!

LETTER

To his former parishioners and friends: A year ago yesterday, I landed in Rio. A year – I can hardly believe it! First of all, my thanks to all of you who have written to me and are praying for me, in la Minotière, la Bastelle, Chesne-les-Monts, at home, and elsewhere. If I don't always answer at once it's only for lack of time. My thanks too to those who have decided to form a group of lay mission helpers. It's a marvellous work... As you know, there are three objects for such a group: the support of friendship, spiritual support and material support. All three are needed. It is the Church as a whole that is missionary, not just a few mad adventurers – or rather, we are all invited by Christ to live daily the madness of the gospel, and get daily more deeply involved in the adventure of building the kingdom of God.

It's hard to know what to say about myself, my daily life, my joys and my problems. These first seven months working in the north-east have been filled with discovery and new friends. So many visits to people's homes, our own community life of laymen and priests, our shared anxiety for the apostolate, these are the essential elements in the framework of my day-to-day existence. I am gradually becoming most involved in the ACO – Catholic workers' groups – and thus tending to leave my parish more often, to take part in various meetings in different parts of the city, to visit the homes of the group leaders, and to help in the formation of new teams. We have at present for the city of S. two foundation teams (all active members), and five progress teams (of beginners) who meet regularly (that is, once a week). Almost all of my evenings are taken up by the ACO. Once a month we have a study day in a remote place in the *mato* (the bush) that borders the town. A coordinating team regroups the various ACO leaders twice a month; this team is working mainly on method at the moment – especially as regards rethinking working life, and reflecting upon our social obligations and apostolic responsibilities. The object is to get to grips with the whole of working-class life – with all levels of work, in all districts, and with all the workers' organizations. For this, one thing seems absolutely necessary: to have one, or better still, two permanent staff (one of each sex) who give their full time to the ACO; it's up to us to assure them a living wage.

I have just made a trip through the north-east, which has confirmed me in my intention of working really hard for the ACO. I've come back with my head full of ideas, and above all with a stronger conviction than ever that the hope (and probably the only hope) for the Church in Brazil is to interest, train, support and deeply involve convinced laymen; the old Christian world is over and done with. It's no good dreaming nostalgically of the past – we must look boldly to the future. In the past we had a Church involved in the world, and Christians whose faith was splendid but who had not made the necessary connection between faith and living. In the future, as is clear from the Council, from common sense, and from the spontaneous direction the Church is taking today, we must have a poorer Church that is more evangelical, and concentrates its energy and its powers upon training laymen to be the leaven in this world – a world which, whether we like it or not, will be a pluralist one.

Joaquim, one of our community of priests and laymen, has now given up his job to become a full-time worker for the YCW, which means a big drop in pay for him. We also have a full-time worker for the girls' branch of the movement, Melia; she's been here for a fortnight, and is a simple girl, but with great character, and black as black.

Yves and I are soon to have the pleasure of welcoming in S. two girls from the 'Nest' (a reception centre for prostitutes in Paris, run by a group of Christian women), who are going to work in a working-class district where there are a great many prostitutes (it's a fearful problem here). Later on we shall have the equally great pleasure of welcoming a third French priest who is coming to augment and complete our little team: Fr Richard Desvilles, from a diocese in northern France, who is going to be specially involved in the YCS (Young Christian Students, a group of colleges and high schools). Here in S. there are more than 12,000 school and college students, and only one priest who can give a little time to the YCS girls. Richard will arrive in November, study Portuguese in São Paulo till the end of January, and then come to us (unless he goes to Petrópolis for a course). We want him as soon as we can have him!

Our parish of Piraï gets plenty of visitors; recently there was Archbishop de Milleville, who was expelled from his diocese in Conakry, New Guinea; also M. and Mme Chalet, Belgians, leaders in a lay missionary organization similar to Ad Lucem; Canon Gilles, who teaches at Louvain; Fr Francisco Acarro, from the Mission de France; Michel Perillou, a French YCW staff member sent to Brazil ... to say nothing of innumerable Brazilians.

I don't think, however, that our parish is an example of a classic Christian community. For instance, in seven months I am pretty sure that I've heard the confessions of no more than fifty people. It's hard to believe, since the parish contains about twelve thousand (some certainly go to the next parish, but still ...); and yet the people organize processions without any priest, they have a great devotion to St Joseph, St Sebastian, St Benedict, and of course to Nossa Senhora, our Lady...

At the moment we have neither an archbishop nor an auxiliary: they have gone to the Council, but also we have lost Dom Renaldo who has just been named Archbishop of F... Dom Poletta is a wonderful man, and I only hope he won't be moved as well.

I pray for you; please pray for me. My love to you all. May the peace and joy of the Lord be with us all, always !

LETTER

To his parents: So, we have lost Aunt Denise – or rather she has gone ahead of us. It won't be so long before we see her again. . .

Here things are not drawn out. You decide to die at eight in the evening; the next morning – only a few hours later – your body is in the ground in the cemetery; for here, things are very primitive. There are no vaults, and the coffins are made of very thin wood, like orange boxes. The only thing I don't like is the business of photographs which seems to me quite horrible, and clean contrary to belief in the resurrection of the body. They come out of the undertakers and open the coffin : photos. They get to the cemetery and open it again : photos. The same performance is repeated by the grave. It is very odd how the mentality of simple people is made up of a mixture of genuine faith and pagan practices. For instance, the evening before the burial, all the young people of the area meet at the dead person's house and spend the night playing, singing, drinking, etc. I don't think they actually dance, but they might just as well. The other day, when I arrived to say some prayers over a dead woman, they were having such a good time that I had to ask for a few minutes' silence. The group of young people outside, and the dead woman's brother, a YCW member, greeted me with joyful cries of 'Padre Paolo' – in the same tones they might use to say, 'I've just won a million.' For them it's an ordinary event. Death seems far closer to them than it is for people at home who will do all they can to avoid using the word, and yet will spend so much money and trouble fighting against it and keeping it at a distance. I would have said that people here have a basically pagan attitude, yet which of the two is really the more pagan? Does not our unhealthy fear of death conceal a selfish wish to enjoy this life, a refusal to accept the most important dimension of all – the spiritual dimension of life?

I got Father's letter first, then Monique's. Yes Father: I'll say mass for Aunt Denise as soon as I can. When our parishioners come to ask for a mass it's always free; if they want they can bring a small offering at the offertory. You can do the same if you like: I have everything I need. Let us hope the Council will put an end to the scandal of our 'scale of charges', bringing money-making right into our churches. Good God, do they think you can sell the blood of Christ? ... If one had to choose, I'd rather see priests dying of hunger (starting with the fattest ones!) but it won't come to that just yet.

End of joke. My thanks also to Marie-Lou for her wonderful letter; I'm carrying it in my heart, like a tune which finds an echo inside me; I'll write back soon. 'Soon' – you know what that means! It's used a lot here, as also is that other useful word, 'perhaps'.

Monique, what you have achieved is terrific ... this group of lay auxiliaries now eighty strong, the coordination between our town, la Minotière, la Bastelle and even Verguy. Please congratulate all the organizers and give them my warmest thanks. Beyond the individual priests you help and support, there is a tremendous value in this awakening missionary spirit, this movement (which corresponds to the direction of the Council) to widen the catholic, i.e. universal, perspective of our faith.

Bernard and Jean-Yves, how are the jobs going? You should come here, and begin to teach people how to plant and water and grow things. It's incredible; of course the lack of money explains the desperate lack of vitamins and calories in the food, but there is also, and more important, a lack of knowledge. The mentality of the people who are farming in the north-east is still back with the Indians, and the African bushmen. They gather what grows wild, but they don't plant or cultivate – or hardly at all. And here, but with all my love, I must stop.

DIARY

Here in S. we have everything, but very little of it.

It's almost impossible to get into hospital. One sick man was refused admittance. Yet there were seven beds free. They said 'There's no room,' yet they can always find room when they want to. So this man went in, got into a bed and stayed there. The nurses didn't dare remove him. The next day the doctor came past; he saw him and told him to go, to go home : if he would only wait for a short time, they'd send for him. He went and he waited, but no one came. So during the night he returned to the hospital, and lay down across the doctor's door so that he couldn't go into his house. When the doctor got there his wife opened the door, and said 'Let him come in.' So the doctor let him in, and finally signed an admission slip for him to go into hospital.

Two girls I met in one house had seven complete collections of heart-throb magazines of the *True Confessions* type. Illusion is the daily bread of these and so many others.

Nearly all the couples in 'Brasília' are unmarried. All the huts (between 350 and 400) are built on stilts in the sea, in the mud. And they are gradually sinking into the sea. People say that in three or four years each house sinks five or six feet, and then they have to build a new one.

Three sick adults in the same street : one asthmatic and two consumptives. And many sick children, especially with eye-trouble, swollen stomachs, etc.

The humidity is appalling.

One carpenter has found a livelihood: with the wood from orange-boxes, he makes trunks and suitcases – they're rudimentary, but they are suitcases. He has five children. Another man sells odds and ends by the roadside. He has seven children.

In one house there live a coal-merchant and a mason, and both pay their rent on the same day. But the mason is out of work at the moment, and the landlady let him put off payment. The coal-merchant was furiously jealous and the two men attacked each other with knives. The landlady was frightened out of her wits and actually became ill as a result!

Itapecerica da Serra
8 January 1964

LETTER

To his family and friends: Happy Christmas to every one of you. And many thanks to every one who has sent me New Year wishes. Thank you for your friendship, your sympathy and your prayers. I simply haven't the time to answer every one, but this letter brings all the affection I feel for each and every one of you...

I'm writing this time from a place just under twenty miles from São Paulo; Fr Yves and I are having a retreat and a holiday, which is doing us a great deal of good.

We are much struck by the difference between this São Paulo area and our own state, S. They're enormously different, in every way. Above all, the standard of living is far higher here – there just isn't the same appalling poverty as in the north-east... There is the closeness of São Paulo, which is a constantly expanding industrial centre. The level of humanity and culture is far higher too, so that, even in the most remote part, the *sertao*, there is a lot of cultivation, whereas S. is still practically in the stone age (though even here the area under cultivation is ridiculously small).

73

At present it is summer, but it is far cooler than in S. In fact S. is not much nearer to São Paulo than Moscow is to Paris, and Itapecerica is over 1,000 feet above sea level.

From the Christian point of view, things seem very promising, yet it must be admitted that the Church is still tragically in need.

I want to tell you now about our work in the north-east. After our first very active ten months, Yves in the parish of Conceiçao and I in Piraï, the bishop is going to give us a new parish, Santa Teresinha. It is a very poor parish indeed, and has to all intents and purposes no priest...

We got this news in a letter from Dom Poletta, our auxiliary bishop. We shall be a team of three: Fr Yves, myself and Fr Richard Desvilles who has just arrived in Brazil.

Yves will be most directly responsible for the work of the parish. Richard will be involved with the YCS for the whole city (the school population is between fourteen and sixteen thousand), because he has a lot of experience with this work. And I shall mainly be occupied with the ACO in the city.

We're delighted that we shall be in a team together. I know Santa Teresinha slightly – it is very like Piraï, being also part of the 'poverty belt' of the city. But I'll tell you more about it when I know it better... I know we have a fairly large church up on the hill that dominates S., but there's no presbytery, only one room where we can sling our hammocks till we get something better. Pray for me.

I'm very sad to be leaving my parishioners in Piraï. We've got to know one another pretty well, and become good friends: I've visited almost every one of their houses. And it's sad to be leaving Lucio, Joaquim and Jose Fernandez too... But it's the will of God, and we are all children who have put our hands into the hand of our Father. And all the poor, wherever they are, are part of one big family.

Yves and I are to leave Itapecerica for Rio on 14 January: we'll meet Richard when he disembarks from the *Charles*

Tellier. Then he's off to Petrópolis for his training course, and we'll go back to S., stopping on the way for a week in Recife to take part in the first conference on the working-class apostolate for priests of working-class parishes, and chaplains or future chaplains of the YCW and the ACO.

The economic, social and political situation in Brazil remains explosive... The outlook of the people of the north-east is certainly very fatalistic in general, but there's no saying what this may lead to... You would say they had reached the limit in poverty – yet life continues to get inexorably more expensive, and wages remain ridiculously low: the minimum salary in S. is still 12,000 cruzeiros (now only 20 dollars) whereas in the state of São Paulo it is 21,000. The price of a great many things has doubled, trebled and even quadrupled in the past year. In Piraï and other working-class districts of S. cooking oil is sold, not by the bottle, but by the spoonful; and cigarettes are sold singly. I've never seen salad or fresh vegetables on my parishioners' tables – they cost too much; all they eat is rice, cassava flour (extremely indigestible), a little fish and very occasionally meat. Very little fruit – only a very few bananas and oranges. A great many people have only one meal a day, and make do in the evening with some cassava flour in their coffee. Along with this material poverty goes considerable backwardness in culture and technology. For instance, almost no one takes advantage of his back-yard to put in some vegetables, though the ground is good and there's enough water. Thus they almost never have green vegetables, and yet a Japanese colony not forty miles away have managed to grow all varieties of vegetables very successfully – though they can't market them because there are no roads or railways!

Another example is the terrible lack of hygiene... Almost all my parishioners eat with their hands; I know one social worker who does the same sometimes. When I spend a day of recollection with the ACO leaders, when it comes to lunchtime, *almoco*, I'm the only one who uses a spoon and a knife. Adults find it quite normal to spit in the kitchen, and children pee on the floor. Handkerchiefs don't exist; people blow their noses either on their shirts, or the bottom of their skirts (elegantly raised for the purpose). The W.C.s (if you can even call them that) are primitive in the extreme, and often right next to the kitchen. The drinking water is seldom filtered (though this is an absolute necessity). Pigs roam at will in the so-called streets, wraith-like dogs gather into wild packs at night, and frequently kill each other in their fighting. Illness is everywhere: tuberculosis, malaria, eye diseases (there are a lot of blind people, and a lot more who will be), intestinal diseases, and of course, anaemia, due to under-nourishment. No doctor ever gets as far as us, partly because there are no roads for cars to drive on, and partly because no one could afford to pay for a visit. And even when people go, in really desperate cases, and queue from six in the morning until midday for a free medical consultation in a public centre, they come home with a prescription they can't afford to get made up.

And the moral misery... The other day a woman had an argument with her neighbour, so she went to get her *façao* (big knife) and killed her with one blow to the heart.

In Piraï seven or eight per cent of the people are married civilly, and another three or four per cent in church. Most women and girls live with one man for a while, and then with another. What we call prostitution in France is the norm here; but you can't really call it prostitution, for it has no moral significance; it's simply that in a sub-human situation it is impossible for a normal, stable family life to survive.

I could go on endlessly and never tell you all there is to tell about this poverty which is our everyday setting. You can't ever get used to it. Yet there's so little one can do. We've got to transform the whole political structure, make a social revolution, develop industry, provide work, provide education. No one can do all this. But the little that one priest can do is still a lot: making the Church present among them; calling communities into being; gradually training leaders; sowing the seed of Christ – Christ in his passion but also in his resurrection. It is true that suffering is never wasted (there are genuine Christian values in the love, and even the joy with which many of them face their poverty); but we have also got to help the people to get rid of their horrible pagan fatalism. I always say to them, 'It's true, Jesus was born poor, lived poor, and died poor; he loved poverty. But he always fought against suffering. You have no right just to accept it. You *must* unite to fight together against suffering.'

Note, however, that a tourist spending a few hours in S., walking round the city centre, would have no idea of this suffering (apart from a few unmistakable signs like ragged shirts, innumerable beggars, and ancient buses fit only for the scrap heap). There's one street of shops where you can buy almost anything; the airport is putting up new buildings ten storeys high. There are quite a few middle-class people, an 'aristocracy of wealth', who live in attractive villas only a few hundred yards away from our filthy stilt-houses, and who know almost nothing of the poverty in them – at any rate they never come to see.

At present it's summer, which means that it's still as hot as ever, but now there's no rain. Even when it does rain everyone stays in just shirts; raincoats are almost unheard of – you couldn't wear one in this heat anyhow. Umbrellas, on the other hand, reign supreme. I don't know what all the umbrella-makers are waiting for – they could make their fortune here...

Don't think that my daily lot consists of unrelieved poverty. There is joy too. The joy of belonging to Christ forever. The joy of the priesthood and of a heart that grows younger every day ... the joy of having responded to Pope

John's call for Latin America. The joy, above and beyond everything, of unconquered, unconquerable hope.

My thanks to all those who have written to me. I've already had one communal letter from the lay mission helpers in la Minotière. My thanks, too, to all those who have so kindly sent me money through my father.

Pray for me, pray for us. We're a poor lot, but we're part of a Church sitting in Council. For you too, things are on the move. We are hand in hand.

Happy New Year! The peace of the Lord be with you.

S., 25 January 1964

LETTER

To his sister and brother-in-law: Today is Saturday; I'm writing this evening from the home of the Canadians, a quarter of an hour's walk from my new parish. Tomorrow I take up my new post officially in the evening during the four-thirty mass, and Dom Poletta will be there. But we've already begun to get in touch with people in Santa Teresinha. Since we have no presbytery, we're going to live in a little rented house till we can get the necessary work done to make the room behind the church habitable. Santa Teresinha is a very friendly district. It was certainly dreadfully sad to leave Piraï, and I did so with many *saudades* (an untranslatable word meaning something like regret and nostalgia). Yves feels the same about his parish; but I'll still have quite a few opportunities to go back there, because there are ACO groups in every district and I'll be continually going back and forth in the city, giving more and more time to the work. I'm certainly not completely up to the job, but all I can do is my best. It's difficult: you need a lot of patience and hope (I suppose they're really the same thing), because there's so little human material to work with; the people are so poor in every sense and, also, they are so wedded to their complete poverty (it's no love match, but it's their only means of survival) that it's a long process getting them to fight against it and stirring up any spirit of revolt (the revolution of the gospel).

Yesterday, when I got home from a meeting at eleven in the evening, I found a woman of thirty or so lying on the ground, on the pavement, with two children. She was dying. Two local women, one an ACO leader, went to see the doctor in charge of the hospital, but he couldn't take her – he had no room. After an hour's argument, she went to the hospital just the same. When she got there, there wasn't a single bed. At last they did attend to her but she died all the same – not from lack of medical attention, but simply from hunger...

I was glad to get your letter yesterday, because I'd had no news at all from home for six weeks, except for the parcel and money that Dom Poletta passed on to me the other day.

What a lot there will be to say when we meet... To think that I once had a dog called Gitan, and budgerigars that died because I gave them too much cheese! ...

Part 3
The Lord is there
ahead of us in
people's hearts

DIARY

The girls who sell tickets on the buses earn a miserable 8,000 cruzeiros a month (just over 13 dollars). Seven hours' work a day, from six till one, or from one till eight or nine in the evening. The conductresses in the *kombis* * have a ghastly time – jolted, never able to stand up straight, squeezing past the passengers because there's so little room.

I chatted with some people who were waiting for a bus. They were waiting for a bus, and I was going to go by *kombi* (which is rather dearer) because I was in a hurry: 'You're going with the rich; we're waiting for the poor man's transport.'

In São Jose Street, a young man with heart trouble collapsed on the ground. The whole street went into action as a real community; they knew just how poor he was, because he had no friends, no family, no money. It was Christ passing by, I think.

What is the Church to say to this woman? She's living with a man who has three wives at once. He married the first, though not in church. Now he spends one day with one, another with another. She looked very sad. She said, 'I'm not very happy; for instance, I've had no dinner today.' We chatted about the unity between man and wife in a home and what it means in natural law and in the law of God.

Two workers in one of the fibre factories in S. are forever quarrelling. One of them feels a particular dislike for the other, though she said, 'I know it's awful, and I know it's my fault.' The other day she said, 'If I had a knife I'd kill her.' It's inevitable for people to get like this – not just because they've had no Christian training, but because of the working conditions in the factory: the noise is appalling, and the dust; they have to work at terrific speed if they aren't to lose even the meagre wage they get; and they're on their feet all day.

* Volkswagen minibuses – one type of public transport, rather dearer than ordinary buses.

LETTER

To his parents: I'm writing in the midst of a jumble of trunks, cases, and filthy old sticks of furniture; it's our sacristy, but also our dining room, parish hall, drawing room and dormitory – at least we're putting up our hammocks to sleep here tonight. Up to now we've slept upstairs, in a vast room full of dust and draughts. But workmen are coming to divide that into three bedrooms for the three of us tramps who will be living here. At the moment there are only two of us, because Richard's still at Petrópolis.

We're lucky. A *velinha* (old woman) brings us our food every day. Our house is always full of people – they come out of curiosity at a novelty. The Fathers who have arrived here are a big attraction. A whole army of good churchwomen – some fat, some skinny – come several times a day to scrape the cement floor of our 'palace' to demonstrate their pleasure that we have come. Quite a success, you see.

It's a cushy job because we've got a church. But we have absolutely no toilet arrangements. Yves always declares that I don't have these human needs, but alas... Luckily, a boy has given us a key to a nearby school building where there are the necessary facilities !

Our church is a large building, roughly ninety feet by forty, it has four walls and an altar where you can say mass facing the people, a crucifix and a statue of St Thérèse. What more could one want?

1 *February:* I was interrupted the other day. I spent yesterday among the streets of my new neighbourhood. I've changed my method of visiting : rather than going systematically from door to door, I go through as many streets as I can, and whenever I see someone standing outside a door, or a man working inside, I start chatting, and then go inside.

The leader of the Assembleia de Deus (they're Adventists, rather like Jehovah's witnesses) has asked me to their service this afternoon : 'It will be a great honour for us,' he said.

I was asked for some holy water, which was undoubtedly going to be used as a 'cure' for something. 'I'm afraid I can't bless any water until Easter.' (What a lie !) Further along I came to a household of consumptives, where one old man is gradually dying. Tomorrow I shall take him communion. A *carrosseiro* (driver of a little donkey cart – there are lots of them here) called gaily, 'Yes it is, it's the Father who was in Piraï !' I went into a snack bar to have a 'cola-jesus' – a horrible fizzy drink, but at least it's cold; we chatted. This is my little world; and it's wonderful – I love it. And I think they realize that. These are the kind of simple people Christ must have known in Palestine...

But I must admit that it's taken a lot of tenacity to get this letter written. The church is never empty of people coming and going; they come to call on the Padres. At this very moment a gaping crowd is watching me as I type. The workmen come and go, with hands full of nails, talking about how expensive life is and how awful it is to be so poor. Delegations have come from João Bello and Piraï to beg us to go back with them to our old parishes. They tell us they've had petitions signed.

Our two masses at six in the morning and six in the evening, are very well attended. They've learnt quite a lot of hymns already.

Fortunately we did not go to live in the house called *Do Menino Jesus* (The house of the Child Jesus) where we were offered rooms to rent; it's a brothel in fact (but of course that's quite common here). In most such houses there are quantities of pictures of saints, and statues with candles or vigil lights burning in front of them. Some prostitutes even make novenas or 'promises' to our Lady, asking her to get them work ! Who would cast the first stone ? That is what real poverty means. You exploit every possibility of earning a few cruzeiros rather than starve or let your children starve.

Tomorrow I'm going to an ACO study day. Almost every evening there's some group meeting, either an established team, or a group of beginners. This evening I'm going to the meeting of the Uniao dos Moradores (union of neighbourhood communities).

I really must stop. Pray for me. I can't tell you how happy we are, but one must move slowly, which calls for patience and love. These at least the Lord will supply.

DIARY
Reflections on the mentality of the people
1. Signs of paganism:
Stars on the doors of the houses – *Macumbas*.
No fathers – just women bringing up children.
Prostitution.
People throw a spadeful of earth on to the coffin to ward off bad luck.
Pictures of naked women all over the walls.

One day a prostitute asked me, 'Why can't a prostitute be a godmother?' I tried to explain, and she finally said, 'Oh, yes, priests won't allow people to be godmothers with short sleeves, either, they must have long sleeves.'

The kind of devotion to the saints practised here is syncretism. There are many signs that the influence of Africa is still very much alive: for instance, polygamy isn't *just* the effect of poverty.

There's a house where the prostitutes can go to get rid of their babies when they're three or four months pregnant. It costs 5,000 cruzeiros (just over 8 dollars) without anaesthetic, 10,000 with.

You often hear people say, 'Life is just this, life is this world; there is not any other.'

The other day a carpenter said to me, 'After reincarnation (it's the spiritists who believe in reincarnation) I don't want to be a carpenter any more, because I'm always making nice furniture for other people, and I only have rotten stuff at home. And it's a trade you can't practise honestly.'

The other day, we were in the middle of a May procession when we met another procession in the same street: it was the Divino Espirito Santo, the Divine Holy Spirit – a kind of half-pagan, half-folklore society.

In one house where spirits are worshipped this is what I saw: five bowls of water on one table; five other bowls: one in the middle of the room and one in each corner; a mass of white flowers, stars, a big framed picture of a woman with long hair and a star in her hand walking on the sea; in another corner, a framed Sacred Heart. There's syncretism for you! When she came out, the woman who runs this spiritist house, and who the neighbours tell me is a spirit-healer, declared: 'We are Catholics.'

The reason why people ask for holy water (which they do constantly) is to use it for healing as they are taught.

The *Macumba*: one day a woman told me: 'Well yes, in the world there are two spirits at work. The spirit from below who does harm, you've got to watch out for him; the spirit from above who gives us everything good.'

II. Signs of genuine faith:

In 'Brasília' one day I met a mother who was in tears. Her little boy had just died; but her eyes lit up as she added, 'I'm sure he didn't die as a pagan.'

It seems to be quite common for people to see Christ in the person of beggars. You often feel, from their attitude and what they say, that their response to poverty is bound up with love of Christ.

There is an ambivalence in what they call here 'conformism': it means something akin to 'fatalism', but they never actually say 'fatalism', always 'conformism'. For instance when they say, '*E preciso se conformar*,' what they mean is, 'We must accept it.' You often hear them say, 'We must accept, we must conform to the will of God.' But it's an ambivalent expression : there is something pagan in this outlook of passivity, fatality, inertia; yet there is also something Christian that you often sense too – an acceptance of the cross, and a profound faith and hope in spite of everything.

At one time the people of Riobamba thought the priests were going to take away 'their' statue, to which a lot of people make pilgrimages, and they made the most violent efforts to prevent the jeep the priests were in from getting through because they (quite wrongly) thought that was what they had come for. There was certainly an element of the pagan – of superstition and fanaticism – in their behaviour, but there was a Christian attitude too. They were saying, 'No one, not even the priests, can take our statue away. No one can take away our faith.' You really get the impression here that in one sense religion is not the priests, but the people.

One Christian worker says, 'I used never to have time to do anything, to go to mass, or work with my mates. Now I do find the time. Why?'

Another ACO leader : 'When I was at the first meeting of the movement (which took place in my home) I stayed in the hammock complaining that I was ill. It wasn't true. Today I can't bear to miss a single meeting. Christ has beaten me.' (Those were his actual words.)

When there is danger of death and no priest available, the people generally will baptize their dying babies themselves at home. There's usually someone in the street who's recognized as being good at it, and they go to find that person, because everyone says, 'You can't let him die a pagan.'

You often hear something like this : 'I was born in the Catholic faith and I want to die in it.' Quite often the fact of leaving the Catholic Church to join a Protestant Church or sect may well be a tribute to the Catholic Church. A tribute because of the reasons which underlie the act: with a kind of common sense of the faith, they can no longer accept a devotion to the saints which is in fact, though not in theory, false (in fact it is a form of idolatory as practised here).

III. Notes on culture:
In theory there is no colour prejudice. Yet, you get the odd hint of it. The other day a catechist said to me, 'The white girls won't talk to the coloured ones.'

They haven't the same idea of the family meal as we have (at least among the sub-proletariat): they hardly ever all eat a meal together. Usually the women serve the men and the guests, and themselves eat standing up in the kitchen.

One thing that is very characteristic is a respect for life. For instance, dogs. There are masses of dogs. The people say, 'What we have most of round here is children and dogs.' They'll never finish a dog off, kill one, even if it's dying. They let them die of themselves.

Another very common trait: it often seems to me that though they have not yet achieved the 'supernatural', these people are deeply 'natural', in other words, human. There is a firm base of humanity which often seems no longer to exist in societies we call 'developed' – for whom the 'supernatural' is often a kind of papering over a non-existent wall. Here on the contrary there is a genuine wall, and it's solid. All that is lacking is the grace to illuminate and consecrate it.

At home, when a road is being repaired, you see signs saying: 'Warning: roadworks'. Here in Brazil they read: 'Attention: men at work.' This seems to be pretty typical of the difference: we see the technological aspect of work being done, where they see men labouring who could be run over by a careless driver.

One sign of faith is how often you see religious inscriptions on houses, buses and even donkey-carts. 'God guide you,' for instance, or, 'Do good, no matter to whom,' or, 'God gives the orders here,' or, 'I am the driver of this car, but the guide is God,' or, 'God may be slow, but he never fails to come.'

S., 15 February 1964

LETTER

To his former parishioners and friends: 'The Carnival is over, the roses will soon bloom...' This floated into my head as I began this letter. Yes, the Mardi Gras is over, and we're getting back to normal. The delirium that seizes hold of the whole population has died down. The peace and quiet are heaven after the fantastic screaming of the loudspeakers and the hurly-burly in the streets. The whole city was alive with people in masks, shouting, singing and dancing. You had to be extremely careful to avoid being sprayed with the coloured water and talcum powder the children use on everyone going by. I was addressed by a bear, who took off his head to ask me the time – just one among many incidents I haven't the space to describe here.

Yet it did not stop raining once during the three days' carnival, and it's still coming down in torrents. As I write a she-ass and her colt have just come into the church to take shelter – but that is something quite usual here; as also are the half-starved horses that wander freely all over the town, weaving their way among the trams and buses, and the bony dogs who assist piously at mass without any objection from anyone ... to say nothing of mothers breast-feeding their babies – which is after all quite natural! The mass is a great family gathering, and that being so, even tiny babies join in the communion which is the family meal.

I'm beginning to visit everyone in our new parish, a very friendly one. It is divided into two sections: the part close to the road from the airport to the city is called Coraca, and the part behind that is Santa Teresinha. There are somewhere between fourteen and fifteen thousand inhabitants, but it's hard to get an exact figure. We shall soon know more, because a pre-missionary sociological survey is to be carried out over the whole city in October 1964.

There is the same desperate poverty as in Piraï. But the area is much pleasanter – quite attractive in fact : the streets are more spacious; there's still a lot of mud and dirt, but people are less crowded together. Our church stands on a hill from which you can look down on the whole city. There is a little port in the area (used mainly for lumber, cement and bricks), a small rice-processing factory, a radio station and transmission tower, and a modern school block next to the church. The great majority of the houses are made of beaten earth with palm-leaf roofs, but there are some brick houses.

At the moment (though this only matters to a few very well-off people), the electricity fails at least half the time; but in fact very few people have it at all, and all our ACO meetings, which take place in the leaders' houses, are lit by the feeble light of a kerosene lamp contrived out of an old jam tin. Very few houses have any water, and in any case it is turned on for only a few hours a day; all day you see a procession of women and children going to the well; you can imagine what a problem laundry is! Though it's a graceful sight to see a woman carrying a heavy water-tin on her head (they carry everything on their heads here), it is also a sight that represents a horribly inhuman struggle and exhaustion...

After the torrential rain we have been having, the streets have turned into mud-puddles, and some have completely given way. You can't imagine how heavy this rain is : it can change a street beyond recognition in twenty-four hours. For instance, the other day I went along a street without noticing anything special about it; the next day (last Monday, that is), there was an enormous rift five feet deep, with a flood of muddy water rushing along it. I wasn't watching my step, and down I went; I splashed about at the bottom for several minutes before I could get my breath back, because I'd bashed myself on a stone. The next day, I was X-rayed, but luckily I had nothing worse than a cracked rib. As the captain says (Yves, to wit), 'We aren't paid much, but we do have fun.' Next day I wrote forcefully to the papers about the state of neglect in which the authorities leave the working-class districts – and in three days that particular hole was filled in.

I don't think I told you that after we'd been here in Santa Teresinha for four weeks, we had a little ceremony one Sunday afternoon in which Dom Poletta officially established us in our new post. Yves was extremely cock-a-hoop at being introduced as the parish priest (I only say this to annoy him, for in fact we are a marvellous team of two, and with Richard who we're waiting anxiously for, we'll be three)... Padre Paolo was introduced as his 'cooperator', and as specially concerned with the adult Catholic workers' groups throughout the city.

Our church has no tabernacle, no confessional, no baptistry, no bell, no lightning-conductor, no chairs, no kneelers – just four walls, and holes for windows. Such as it is, it is very attractive, with none of the usual collection of bearded saints, nor the hideous trappings of luxury... We shall gradually fit it out, beginning with the real necessities, and trying to stick to simplicity. When Dom Poletta got back from the Council, he handed over to me the considerable sum which you had collected for me; I can't tell you how useful it will be with all these basic expenses.

The people in the area are delighted to have, for the first time, two priests 'of their own'. In the past a priest used to come just to say mass on Sundays. Each day we have mass at six in the morning and six in the evening, both attended by between fifty and a hundred people, including quite a few men (twenty or so). I'm beginning to teach them some modern hymns, and now, after four weeks, we have very good congregational participation, and the singing is coming on well too (we have the whole of David Julien's mass translated into Portuguese and it is well and truly roared out!). And on Sundays, the church is really full... There are lots of confessions and communions, but there are also lots of adults who've never learnt anything. The other day – to give you an instance of the kind of thing that happens – I was sitting outside a house chatting with the people... Neighbours gradually joined us, and I was asked question after question – it became a kind of grown-ups' catechism class...

Most of our people come from the remote country, and have hardly ever had a chance to meet a priest or a catechist, or even to go to church... They hunger and thirst for God. The two chief needs in Brazil seem to us more and more to be the development among all the laity of an awareness of their part in the Church and adult instruction (at a popular level). We have one regular catechist here, now undergoing two months' training, and we are hoping, as a matter of simple justice, to be able to assure her a minimum wage.

There seem to be some influences here that are favourable to the kingdom of God, others the reverse... There is great warmth of heart and generosity on the positive side. But there is this appalling poverty which is always at the root of all spiritual poverty – as exemplified in the *cachaça* (sugar-cane liquor) which they drink in order to forget, and prostitution, which is an economic and psychological phenomenon here, rather than a moral one.

One small example will indicate the kind of climate a priest lives in here. Shortly after we got here, I was visiting in one street when a young woman stopped me and said, 'It's my ambition to marry a priest' – and the look on her face left one in no doubt as to her meaning. I tried to respond with calm good humour and did my best to make her think in terms of the love of God.

It's a peculiar atmosphere – not immoral, but totally amoral...

They are very human, with a great sense of family, and it seems to me that they're more open-hearted than we are in France; they love children, they have a great respect for life... I don't see any basic badness here, but a lack, an emptiness, an appeal, a waiting for something... I find the 'nature' of the people here so 'rich' that it will be wonderfully fertile ground for the supernatural to flourish in when Christ is grafted upon the wild plants that grow there now. Yesterday evening, we were talking about this at the end of a study session with the ACO team from Macauba: how Christ always hated sin, but ardently loved the sinner... And that is what we must do too. God is at work in the heart of the greatest sinners...

Thérèse and Bernadette (the two girls from the 'Nest') are beginning to explore the centres of prostitution. We see them from time to time, and their work will be coordinated with that of the ACO.

Also, some of the women ACO leaders are setting up, with a group of girls and women, an 'Association' of domestic servants eventually to become a trade union... This is one of the worst-off occupations where there is dreadful injustice: wages, working conditions, living conditions, hours, food, treatment, etc. Think of it, lots of *domesticas* only get 2,000 cruzeiros a month (just over 3 dollars). Of course they get their food thrown in, but 2,000 cruzeiros barely pays for a month's transport.

Monday 17 February. I was interrupted the day before yesterday, but here I am again. Our diocese has been struck by tragedy. This week, within five days, two priests in S. have died suddenly. They had important responsibilities in the Church in the north-east... Our lack of priests is getting more and more desperate. There are seventeen *municipes* without priests – and a *municipe* is often bigger than a *département* in France, with over a hundred thousand inhabitants.

Yesterday I think the whole city was at Padre Alfredo's funeral. He was parish priest of the cathedral. It was a fantastic sight: not so much a ceremony as a popular demonstration – from the richest to the poorest. They cried, they prayed; there was genuine faith among them and a tide of human warmth which seems to me the great quality of Brazil.

Priests aren't respected here: they are loved. They are part of the family. But this isn't the least of the many paradoxes in this country: they love the priest, especially when they feel him to be a 'real' priest (the soul of these people is deeply religious), yet there are very few vocations, and I doubt whether many families want any of their sons to be priests... But I haven't time to go into details on this important point. The fact is that we still have no archbishop, that our diocese has fewer and fewer native priests, and that the next priest to be ordained – *if* he perseveres – will not be ready until 1967. Dom Poletta was deeply distressed about the situation when we saw him yesterday.

So please, all of you, pray for us... Thank you, all who have written, and please forgive me for not replying. Life is exciting – I hope you feel the same as you get up each morning? We have to accept the ancient wisdom of the Brazilian people; they are a wise people and a wild people, a childlike people who will throng the streets one week to dance in the Mardi Gras Carnival, and the next to mourn a priest who has died: *Muito, sem Deus é nada, mas pouco com Deus é muito* – 'A lot, without God, is nothing, but a little, with God, is a lot'.

LETTER

To his family: It's the rainy season with us now, and the roads out of here are often absolute quagmires. I am dividing my time between the ACO and the parish. I visit a great deal. We have now two full-time ACO workers, which is a great help. Their first year must be chiefly one of formation. To put you in the picture, I'll just tell you that my full-time man (aged about thirty-five) has only been able to read and write for a year, but he is both generous and intelligent – not the speculative intelligence of middle-class culture, but the practical intelligence of working-class common sense. My girl-worker is a dressmaker, also thirty-five, a widow, a marvellous person and much liked, with great influence in her neighbourhood.

A group of young people came to ask me to be 'their priest'. They are students from the Catholic university group and the MEB, who want a real faith to live by, and who are anxious to meet the demands of Christianity. So I'm spending every Saturday morning with them: we have mass, meditation and discussion.

Yesterday, in half an hour, part of our 'Brasília' was burnt out. More than fifty houses have gone. I went over – they're my former parishioners, and it was hard not to weep. They are the poorest of the poor (you should see what their homes are like) – and what little they did have, they have lost. One child of six was burnt to death, and there are a lot more in hospital. One young woman I'd prepared for marriage showed me her house which I'd visited at the time (and how proud she had been of her few sticks of furniture!). It was burnt to a cinder, even the framed photo of her parents. I left without looking back, terrified that I'd break down and cry. Another woman showed me her burns... One man asked: 'Why isn't it the houses of the rich that get burnt?' The straw roofs blaze up in no time of course. When, oh *when* will the government deal with this cancer of shanty-towns which are a disgrace to the country? – indeed perhaps they're even more of a disgrace to us of the advanced countries. A man explained it to me yesterday in Santa Teresinha, and he's quite right: 'The real reason for our poverty is that the rich countries in America and Europe buy our raw materials and work on them in their factories; so their economy is prosperous and gets richer and richer. They then sell us their manufactured products, which we need: business thrives. All we give in Brazil is our labour and sweat getting the raw materials out of the ground. We shall never get anywhere, because no foreigners want to build up industry here or train local technicians for us to manufacture things ourselves.' Yes, he's right. It's the vicious circle of colonialism and capitalism, an iron collar strangling the country. Unless we have a revolution like Cuba, I can see no hope. I am more and more convinced that the anti-communist myth is something vomited up by the over-fed, a hypocritical defence of the privileged. One can't want communism, because of the materialism that goes with it, but who knows whether the Lord won't make use of it to bring home to us the state of the poor who are crushed beneath our selfishness!

Last Sunday we celebrated Yves's birthday – he's twenty-nine, exactly ten years younger than me. I got everything ready beforehand with some YCW girls, and it went like a bomb. Speeches, singing, cake – we all went slightly mad. I certainly sang *Alouette* with the best of them, and you can hardly sing without dancing a bit too...

A fortnight ago we were visited by Fr François de l'Espinay, our new 'special envoy' from the French Committee for Latin America; he's in charge of all the French priests over here, and is responsible for coordination among us. He went through the whole Algerian war as a chaplain, and is a great man. He spent a week with us, and we were able to swop experiences and do a lot of thinking together.

Our weekday masses are getting better and better, with everyone joining in and singing. We've had a set of thirty-seven hymns printed, almost all modern. The whole neighbourhood say that everything's different since we arrived... On Sundays the church is full to bursting: 'There used to be that many on the feast of Santa Teresinha,' they tell us. But we're under no illusion: we've got to preach the gospel, and we shan't do that simply by filling our church. But there is a real sense of sympathy between us and them, and that should be a help towards evangelizing.

I'd like to say my office in Portuguese, but the breviary in Portuguese isn't to be had yet. Meanwhile, as I'm fed up with the Latin, do you think you could get hold of a second-hand French one for me? I'd be most grateful.

We still have no archbishop, which is a nuisance. Recife has had their archbishop (who died) replaced within a week! They've got Dom Helder Camara, an absolutely outstanding man, who is of course both much loved and much hated, as one should be...

DIARY

The fire in 'Brasília': when I went there did I feel as Christ would have, or did I feel merely human compassion? What would Christ have felt about such a horrible thing? How would he have judged and acted?

One man told me, 'I'm a casual labourer – I earn more that way. I work somewhere different each day. I earn more than I would in a factory, because of their minimum wage...' (that minimum wage which isn't even legal, and certainly doesn't allow of any minimum kind of decent life).

One man of sixty-two has married a girl of about twenty.

Children come to get water and carry it off on their heads; they get ten cruzeiros a tin.

I met a ten-year-old girl: she fetches her neighbours'

water, and the money she earns is used to buy school books. She looks quite worn out, but neither her neighbours nor her parents seem to notice.

I've got to know some Baptists who show clearly this wish the people have to find some link between everyday life (wretchedness, poverty, urgent need) and the Lord who watches over us. And often enough there isn't anyone to help them find it.

I talked to five prostitutes in Cunha Machado Street – we really looked closely at their life: the causes and the consequences of what they are doing. What does Christ think of it? What does he want of them? Just what *is* love? The law of God and our happiness are the same thing. They invited me to dinner with them.

The cobbler in Rua São Jose: his wife takes him his dinner every day on the bus, so he won't lose any working time (or the money that goes with it).

Have met some of the Assembleia de Deus and the Baptists. One girl who works all day and spends the evening studying, has just given her last 200 cruzeiros to the fire-victims of 'Brasília'.

Padre Lucio has an endless struggle, both with simple misunderstanding, and with the machinations of certain politicians.

A widow with three children: she does laundry-work. She lives in a tiny house, and for the past three months she's also had the three children of a woman who was found dying of hunger in the street outside. She's now got the woman herself as well, just released from hospital.

LETTER

To his family: Yes, it seems that there really is a revolution. I certainly want one, but one wonders just what kind of revolution this is. At the moment it sounds more like a right-wing *coup d'état*. The three governors of the states of Minas Gerais, Guanabara (Rio de Janeiro) and São Paulo have apparently succeeded in getting rid of the president of the republic, João Goulart and the few 'slightly' progressive governors, such as Miguel Arrais of Recife and Brizzola of Santa Catarina. But only apparently – because it doesn't seem to be over yet. For the time being, public opinion seems to indicate passive acceptance, especially since the 'promoters' and 'supporters' of the *coup* have managed to turn Jango (i.e. João Goulart) and Miguel Arrais into 'communists'. But I think people have too much sense to be really bamboozled by this : the real reason for the opposition to Goulart is the reforms he had managed to get approved by the general population of Rio at a mass meeting. All we can do is wait and see. Meanwhile, apart from the soldiers guarding all the major strategic points and main roads, things are quiet in S.... Certainly the state of S. will be the last to enter the political juggling in the country – though everyone is glued to the radio, the man in the street doesn't really grasp what is going on.

The first day of the *coup* I went into the street to try and see what people felt, and what I found was interesting. I questioned in turn a soldier of the guard, a bar-keeper, a carpenter, a shop-keeper, an MEB leader and a postal official. I think the most apt comment was made by a poor man who lives near here who walked back with me : 'I don't know much about what's happening, but I do know that people can't take much more. They'll accept any solution, even something quite hopeless, if only things change...'

The miracle is that, Brazil being an essentially peaceable

country, no blood has yet been shed – or almost none. In France there would have been violence long ago. Sometimes when you see the state they live in you're tempted to long for a communist solution, or at least a Castro-type revolution. (Here, public opinion, as formed by the press and radio, brands Castro as a communist.) But the facts speak for themselves, and in the end people will wake up to them. Castro is the only man in Latin America, with all the puppet régimes artificially sustained by the US, who has actually succeeded in ameliorating poverty and under-development; the only man who has begun to fight economic colonialism; the only man who has really tackled illiteracy on any scale – and much else besides. Yet the capitalist powers have forced Fidel into the arms of Krushchev by simply cutting off his livelihood (stopping buying his sugar, the only commodity he has to sell).

This evening, I got back from an ACO meeting in another district, and we reviewed events. What do the workers think of it all? What do we ourselves think? What does Christ think? It's hard to determine... I have a kind of impression that the anti-communist obsession has taken hold among the people, and yet it is hard to see in the attitude of the politicians how much is demagogy and how much any real will to progress.

Sunday 5 April. I've come back to this letter while waiting for the nine o'clock children's meeting (something we began four or five Sundays back, because far too many children were coming to the evening mass which they were really too young to understand). The parish is marvellous, and at present I am in touch with a number of Protestants.

With the 'events' of yesterday, the whole city was in a state of upheaval. The nonsense talked is almost unbelievable. The anti-communist propaganda has been so successful that it is becoming generally accepted: everyone is now talking about a 'communist conspiracy', even the very poor.

LETTER

To his parents: Please don't hold it against me that I don't write oftener. My days are full and overflow into the nights. Each evening there are meetings. I go by *kombi* and generally come back on foot, as it's too late then for anything else – it's often up to an hour's walk. During the day: visits, meetings, all kinds of contacts, preparing conferences; and in addition we have all the material problems involved in our building and alterations. The house is now almost finished, and we've begun on the church, to which some things simply must be done straight away.

Since Corpus Christi we have had another person living with us – a guest of honour who will be here from now on: Jesus. We have actually completed a pretty little chapel inside our hut, and Jesus is sharing our Bohemian way of life. Yves calls him the Boss. The people aren't ready yet for reservation in the church (the church is the people's house, but they don't yet realize that it's God's house too). Meanwhile, they can come and pray before the Blessed Sacrament whenever they like, because our house is always open, and people come and go continually anyhow.

Richard still hasn't come, but we expect him any time. This evening we heard that he had some suitcases stolen on his way through Salvador, while he was out sight-seeing.

Dom Poletta came to Santa Teresinha this afternoon. We spent some pleasant, relaxed hours with him. He's leaving us, you know. He's just been appointed to a diocese in the Ceara – a diocese with only twelve priests! It's hard to think that they aren't just politely retiring him, but everyone assures us that they aren't, and he certainly doesn't say so. He is terrific. We think him one of the greatest bishops in Brazil, or, indeed, all Latin America. A new Archbishop, Dom Marcelo, has just been appointed to S. and will get here in July. He sounds pretty good.

Thursday, 4 June. I'll try to get this letter finished today.

This morning I've finally finished decorating our little chapel : three murals. Yves is delighted. We've started on the outside of the church, beginning with the windows. It's vital to do something, because in the rainy season the church was absolutely flooded. We're going to put in hollow bricks, which let in the light and air, but not the rain. The Church must become poor again, that is to say authentic, simple. In fact, simplicity, authenticity and poverty happen also to be the criteria for beauty. Paul VI has just given a tremendous address to artists – you must read it.

15 June 1964

LETTER

To his former parishioners and friends: It's a long time since I wrote, I know, but you must forgive me; I am submerged in work.

How are you all? Here things are pretty good, both for Yves and for me. We've been in our new parish (Santa Teresinha) six months now. The people are very nice. We're beginning to get to know the neighbourhood well by dint of meeting and visiting all the time. Though there is so much to deplore in the desperate poverty we see all round us, there is also much that is good... If only you could come here you could see it for yourselves. It is so difficult to describe anything at such a distance without being unfair, without leaving out part of the truth – the situation is so totally different from anything we know in France. We ourselves try to look at it with neither the rose-coloured spectacles of the optimist nor the dark glasses of the pessimist : we try to see it with the eyes of faith, and the opportunity of re-examining our lives regularly with our lay leaders (Yves with the YCW, I with the ACO) is the greatest help. I'm also keeping a notebook in which I jot down different things that happen, and I find that useful too. Our 'looking upon them' and our

103

prayer as priests must be a link between the Lord and the people : the Lord who speaks, calls, works in secret (before we even begin to do anything), and the people who live, survive and die, who suffer and hope, who accept or struggle...

I must tell you something about what some of the papers here call 'The April 1 Revolution'... In effect it was a military *coup d'état* which, neither in its preparation nor its accomplishment, had any participation from the people. There were a few days of excitement, and then things returned to peace and quiet, if not positive indifference.

The problems remain unaffected, especially that of poverty. People are rightly asking whether solutions haven't been purposely delayed. We are still in the period of purges. The newspapers (all censored) talk a lot about arrests and the repeal of parliamentary mandates. The two most obvious results of the *Golpe* (coup) have been a violent, almost obsessive, wave of anti-communism and a more and more thorough taking over of all national affairs by the army. In S. too the army has arrested quite a number of people, often for quite arbitrary reasons. There have been cases in which the accusation of 'communist infiltration' was quite evidently ridiculous. For instance, one social worker who was quite beyond suspicion suddenly heard one day that she was on a 'blacklist' of names found among the papers of some Chinese communists arrested in Rio. Catholic groups have not been immune to attack; as one might have expected, the MEB has been disbanded, and its leaders caught up in a web of interrogation and suspicion.

Dom Poletta has asked me to be 'spiritual assistant' to the MEB in S. And I therefore presented myself one day at the military barracks to make clear my support of the leaders being molested, and said, 'I've come to be taken prisoner.' My first interrogation went on for four hours.

A new archbishop has just been appointed to S. and should arrive next month. He is Dom Marcelo. But unquestionably the most important thing that has happened in the north-east is the appointment of Archbishop Helder Camara.

We've had a few special events in the parish. During May, we carried a statue of our Lady through all the streets of the neighbourhood. Each evening we went in procession from street to street, and we had mass in the open air in whichever street we were leaving the statue in for the night. It was a very popular demonstration, and an opportunity to stir up interest, get people involved, and carry out a kind of missionary para-liturgy. We're very pleased with the results. The final evening, in conclusion, we went on a *romaria* (a kind of procession on foot in fulfilment of a promise) as far as Riobamba, a very popular shrine nearly twenty miles out of S. More than a thousand people took part. It was an extraordinary sight to see this crowd, praying, singing hymns, then afterwards singing and dancing their own special north-eastern rhythms, by candle-light, and to the accompaniment of the *foguettes* (fire-crackers, which they absolutely love here). We left Santa Teresinha about eight thirty, and got to Riobamba at four in the morning. Everyone brought something: Yves managed to confiscate ten litres of *cachaça* (sugar-cane liquor) and poured the lot into the ground – no one complained, because it was part of the rules not to bring any alcohol. As for me, I got completely 'sent' by the rhythm, and danced quite a few baions and sambas on the road. It was terrific. But I did pray a bit too...

All night one had a kind of vision of the people of God on the march, the true people. One felt the people's soul expressing itself, suddenly rediscovering its roots (some of them certainly African) and being quite at home in the Church... There is a unique opportunity, and I don't think we priests in Brazil really make the most of it, to help the people to get back in their own special way on the road to God.

Our neighbourhood presents a pretty accurate microcosm of Brazil as a whole in the matter of religion; it can best be described in the one word: syncretism – in other words an extraordinary mixture and interpenetration of all sorts of different religions and beliefs. First of all there are frankly pagan elements, like the 'Drum of Minas' (a kind of *Macumba*) and spiritism, both of which are fairly general, especially in some streets. Then there are things that are neither pagan nor Christian, but simply folklore: old popular traditions which have still got a certain meaning, and rather vague religious motivations, with dances, songs handed down from father to son, costumes and disguises, processions, parties, meals, etc. For instance, we have recently had the feast of the Divino Espirito Santo, with a procession of angels and streamers, and the feast of Santo Antonio; we'll soon have that of São João (St John). These are all very colourful, with masses of pictures and statues.

We then come on to a totally different category, with the *crentes* (believers), which means those who are not Catholics and includes, rather incorrectly, all Protestants. Among them one must set apart the members of the Assembleia de Deus, all of them Adventists, a very widespread sect in Santa Teresinha, who stand out for their firm opposition to the Catholic Church and especially to the worship of saints, which they consider idolatry. To prove their point they continually quote the Bible; they know long sections of it by heart, and interpret it in a very limited – sometimes quite ridiculously limited – fashion. It must be admitted that though their accusation is in theory unfair (there are certainly genuine Catholics who obey the spirit of the Church and are not idolators), in point of fact a great many people who call themselves Catholic act as if they worship something other than Christ. One need only see how big a part is played in popular piety – and especially the kind of worship given them – by such saints as Benedict, Sebastian, John, Cosmas and Damian, George, Teresinha and even Nossa Senhora – in whom our Lady is barely even recognizable any more. Yet you can't condemn people who have never really been properly evangelized. It has not taken us long to become convinced that these people need only a minimum of education and initiation to become capable of authentic faith and a genuinely religious attitude. Indeed there are great qualities of freshness, spontaneity, openness to the supernatural and generosity that we in France have perhaps lost... In a general way, I am convinced that the only thing that makes Protestantism strong in Brazil is the weakness of Catholicism. I have quite a few acquaintances among the *crentes* of the Assembleia de Deus. The other day one of them told me that I would not get to heaven, because no Catholic priest can go there. Not very encouraging! ... Another invited me several times to their regular Saturday worship, yet not long afterwards he insisted that I accept a small offering 'to help us rebuild our church'. You feel at such times that some of them are 'tempted' to discover the Catholic Church, tempted to a certain sympathy with it.

At the end of the list, in its own very special place, I must mention the Baptists. These are genuine Protestants, and are very close to us. Basically there are very few differences between us, and sympathy and mutual understanding come easily. We have constant and pleasant contact with several pastors, and we have adopted some of their extremely attractive hymns.

Such is more or less the religious picture of our neighbourhood. In the midst of it all, it must be said that we are generally liked by everyone.

A catechism committee has been formed, and is beginning to take over the training (in religion and methods of religious teaching) of the teachers in the local schools, state and private (there are innumerable little private schools, and each normally has three lots of students, one in the morning, another in the afternoon and a third in the evening).

We are coming to set more and more store by a committed laity, Yves and I. In the war against poverty, we are often brought in to help in cases of urgent need : it is often impossible to avoid this, yet it grieves us to realize that this puts us –in fact, if not in spirit – into the old paternalist category which will never enable people to become fully human. . . That is why we are so convinced that the only truly evangelical response to poverty is to train lay people who will build the Church by building a better world. . . To support those already engaged in the work, and inspire those not engaged in it to join in – these are our greatest concerns. It isn't easy, but it is the only way that will help these people materially or spiritually.

Yves is giving a lot of his time to the YCW leaders, boys and girls both. My special work, apart from what help I can give to the life of the parish, is to be responsible for the ACO throughout the city. All my evenings, or almost all, are taken up by meetings, and I am gradually working my way round all the outlying areas of S. Now, with the two full-time ACO workers we have had since February, the various teams are getting a lot more support. Two new teams are being formed : one in São Carlos, with the help of Padre Pedro, a Canadian, and one in Santa Teresinha. At the moment we are getting ready for the ACO congress of Brazil, from 12 to 19 July. There will probably be six or seven of us representing the ACO of S. The congress was to have been put off because of the *coup*; now it is taking place after all, but without any publicity.

Our little 'presbytery' is now almost finished; it is very basic. Downstairs is the sacristy, which is also our parish hall, a tiny Blessed Sacrament chapel, and a kitchen. Upstairs, three bedrooms (we each have our own), and a shower-room. We've also got electricity.

Our church is gradually being fitted up. We've had benches made, and two rudimentary confessionals; we've begun on the outside which used to look more like the entrance to a prison, and yesterday we set up a huge cross with an immense curtain behind, and some rather clever (we think) indirect lighting to show it up. We try to get everyone as much involved as we can. They understand why we have put our Lady's statue at the side, so that everyone's attention will be concentrated on Christ's death and resurrection at mass. They know that 'no more artificial flowers will ever enter the church or presbytery' (living flowers symbolize a living religion, whereas an artificial flower symbolizes a religion that is inauthentic, deceptive, dead; something 'too pretty to be real'). They know we have declared war to the death upon lace altar-cloths and decorations. No more statues: they know that we respect the saints, but that we have no right to diminish the witness of simplicity, poverty and authenticity that our church is clearly called to give.

We're delighted to think that the third member of our team, Richard, will be here soon. The last we heard, he was in Recife. We think he'll get here *se Deus quiser* (God willing) in ten days' time. He has travelled from Salvador with some Canadian nuns who went to the course at Petrópolis with him, and who will be brought by lorry to our diocese.

Well, I've certainly written a lot today. I hope these few bits of news will help you to picture us here, and to pray for us. Just think, it's already two years since I left la Bastelle! How time flies...

My thanks to all who are helping me, spiritually and materially: former parishioners, lay leaders, friends, lay mission-helpers.

S., *3 August 1964*

LETTER
To his family: Deus tarda, mas nunca falta; that's what they say here. It means: 'God takes his time, but he never abandons us.' And *Deus é Brasileiro* (God's a Brazilian) – in other words in Brazil one must never despair. I've had several proofs of this already. Today for instance, Yves has just come

back with the post, bringing your Christmas tape-recording. Only eight months for an air-mail parcel to get here! But miracles are coming thick and fast: just last week I got five Christmas presents at once! It was like a dream – and indeed it is a dream of eternal Christmas. Quite a lot of things were missing, because all the bags were open, but I got the books, the toys and the cake (which alas had to go straight into the dustbin).

4 *August:* Back to my letter. I'm just back from a meeting (the first time all our lay Catholic groups have met the new archbishop). It's late and there's a background of drums and mournful singing that will go on all night and stop only at dawn. It's one of the innumerable fiestas of the *bairro* (the neighbourhood), one of the feasts of the *Divino Espirito Santo* (there are several musical groups in different parts of the neighbourhood, each performing on a different day – the feast lasts at least ten days and nights). I've strolled round outside the house and chatted with people: it is all very curious...
Silver-painted wooden swords, altars covered with statues and flowers, a hideously ornate *baldachino* with a girl of seven or eight years old underneath, dressed up like a princess. She sits absolutely still on a throne, with a crown, sceptre, cloak – the lot. Musicians, drummers, singers, attendants, a great many people take part, altogether very curious – indeed quite extraordinary... It's folklore with a sort of religious base to it.

Richard doesn't seem to have got used to this almost continual nocturnal racket yet, nor to the almost total absence of silence during the day either. He seems quite bewildered. It certainly takes a lot of getting used to. Yves and I are quite hardened by now. Personally, nothing can stop me from sleeping, but it's sometimes hard to concentrate, to read, to write, to pray, even to talk, with the continual noise day and night.

There's so much more to tell; for instance about the three abandoned children whose mother had become insane. I came across them in town, and they had no shoes; I managed to get them some. We then made use of the radio to announce that the Padre was looking for parents for them : in the next hour we got ten offers ! ... But I could go on for pages and pages.

I must stop. Have a good holiday, and do relax – Mother looks dreadfully thin in the photos.

DIARY

Twenty. Consumptive. He's been stuck in his hammock for eight months, and there were tears in his eyes as he spoke to me. A wretched, tiny house, an exhausted mother. No money, no hope. Then the TB hospital, quite repellently dirty. And they're so hungry. The patients tell me that after each meal they are as hungry as before. When I went to visit the boy there, I saw the patients in their rooms; they were trying to light a fire on the ground, a little coal and wood fire to boil some rice on. He had seen the doctor once in the fortnight he'd been there, and had almost no attention. He died peacefully. He'd have done better to stay at home; at least he'd have died among his own people.

A woman, aged something over forty; not long ago her house collapsed, and she is now staying with her neighbour, together with her old mother of eighty who is blind and ill. She spends the day begging. I saw her in town today, lying down on the ground, almost like a dog. She seems to have lost all sense of her dignity as a human person. What can one possibly *do*?

A boy of twenty-two. His stomach is swollen and hard, and his face too. He's not seen a doctor yet, only a pharmacist. I told them that the doctor of the Uniao dos Moradores (union of neighbourhood communities) gives up to three consultations free.

Jose, from Ribamar. He's just caught typhoid – hardly surprising when you realize where their water comes from. He's in the isolation ward of the Dutras hospital.

A blind woman, going round begging, with four kids. Her husband has left her. She arrived here from the interior four months ago and has no home. She begged me: 'Find me a home.' What can I do? Can we perhaps build something? How can we move from individual help in these cases to institutional action?

Cachaça: two men, drunk on it, got on a plane. The police came; there was a scuffle and one of the policemen pulled a gun and killed one of them. The other was furiously angry and came to tell me about it. What would Christ do if he were me?

Fares have gone up again. What are the poor going to do? Since we got to S. they've already gone up three times at least. Cola-jesus is up too, and a lot of other things.

A woman whose husband is a driver is left alone for two months at a time. The lorry-trip to São Paulo takes twenty-eight days each way, and then he's only home two or three days before being sent off again.

Another woman's husband works as a mason twenty miles out of S. They only see one another Saturday evening and Sunday, because the bus costs too much for him to come home every day.

Herminia has told me: 'I want to be a nun.'

Transport problem: everyone who works in the Arro direction has to walk as far as the cross-roads (a good half hour each way) – otherwise it means changing buses and paying twice.

Magazines with names like *Caprice*, *With All My Heart*, *Illusion*, *Seduction* provide an escape from life; they offer sentimentality and romance to make up for the hardship of real-life marriage (men are animals).

Maria, our full-time ACO worker, insisted that we

shouldn't do anything to celebrate her birthday, but have a party for the wife of Jose Santos instead.

LETTER

To his parents: So you're back from your holiday in Spain; I hope you're all bursting with health and strength and hope! ...

In a few days, *se Deus quiser* (God willing), I'm off to Rio for the ACO national conference. I'm waiting for an answer from the Brazilian air force – I've asked for a place on a plane on Saturday. The civil airlines have almost doubled their prices since last January. Yves is hoping to join me in Rio, also by an air-force plane.

We've recently had a visit from the national chaplain of the ACO, Padre Paolo, and the national organizer, Joaquim. They spent four most rewarding days with us. We visited the whole area, they met all our leaders and the teams, and on the last evening we had a party for the whole ACO of the city and sympathizers; it was great.

Yesterday we had a very successful study day. The new bishop seems to set great store by the laity and has great hopes for what it can do, so though we've lost Dom Poletta, we still have official support from our bishop. I am very much taken up with this training of the laity, but it does create certain problems as far as our team here is concerned. I'm out almost all the time, and only get back very late at night. And I think it's very important to keep in contact with home base, as it were, through the parish. Yves agrees that I should have no official parochial 'responsibilities', but that I should simply keep in touch with people, particularly by house-to-house visiting.

Things are pretty good, as you see. I feel remarkably well, and I'll write again soon.

LETTER

To his parents: A note from Quixada, hoping you got my last letter which will have told you how I got here. I'm having a marvellous holiday. It's a glorious spot, overlooking the Serra, which are something like the Rocky Mountains as seen in westerns, also a bit like Provence with everything burnt by the summer sun, and a bit like Brittany, and a bit like Switzerland! Quixada itself (pronounced 'kishada') is a little town with that sun-battered appearance you find in southern Italy or Sicily. Every day I go for long walks along the hundreds of little mountain paths that wind away to the *mato*. I walk for hours and hours, all day. I've become an enthusiastic walker – I find it a real relaxation. I visit people in the most isolated houses and talk to them: it's fascinating how you get to know people's outlook and their problems. The nuns here are a bit alarmed by me; they think me too adventurous altogether, but I tell them that I'm a rational animal who's still a bit wild. There are other priests on holiday here, some Brazilian, one German, and an Austrian. The most recent arrival, the Austrian, works in the vicariate (i.e. not yet a diocese) of Ximbu. It's in the territory of Para, near the Amazon. They have six priests plus a bishop for an area the size of Italy. True, there are only thirty-four thousand people, but communications are almost non-existent: the only way of getting to the Indians in the interior is by boat. This man is thirty-five, and has just had malaria; I like him very much. There's also a young deacon here from Fortaleza – I've written to Monique about him, because he asked if I could get him some cards for his ordination.

The people here are much more energetic and ready to fight for what they want than the people in S. state; indeed the whole area, both town and country, is far more advanced than ours. Yet you find the same contradictions and anomalies here – for instance in their attitude to farming. It's heartbreaking. They are still at the stage of what I can only call the scorched earth policy: each peasant chooses a spot on the *mato* to grow cotton or *milho* (maize), or *feijao* (black beans), or *mendioca* (cassava): he cuts down all the trees and clears the land; a fortnight later he burns off; then he plants. The first year he gets a good yield, the second much less, the third nothing at all. The ground is finished. So he leaves that spot and moves on to another, with the result that gradually the whole area is being eroded. And I've not seen anywhere in Brazil a plough or any kind of working animal; they all use an archaic implement rather like a hoe. They've never thought of growing cattle-feed. When I think that in S. state, where the soil is so good, sunny and well-watered, people only grow a few poor vegetables in a sort of suspended box (suspended to keep the insects away) never more than one or two yards square! And that will be their greens for a year.

At present there's a conference taking place in the house here of ANCAR, an official organization of volunteers for training people in community and rural awareness. Its object is to transform rural structures and ideas. It's hard work, because the attack has to be made on so many fronts at once. A very nice young American couple from the Peace Corps is taking part.

Between walks, I am immersed in the works of Emmanuel Mounier – very exciting. I'm taking advantage of the silence here to do some real thinking. I'm also much thrilled by Teilhard de Chardin, and am having some most interesting talks with the other priests and lay people here.

How are you all? How I wish you could be with me here for a few days.

Friction in the 'neighbourhood union'.

The union commission went to discuss the transport problem with the Prefect. The Prefect is afraid of the people, and would not meet the whole commission; he received four of them after keeping them waiting an hour and a half.

A woman from the Lari district. She can't put her marriage right, and has eight children. She's ill and mentally unstable and wanted to commit suicide. The priest told her she couldn't have absolution, so she left in despair.

A woman who has belonged to the Adventists since she was a small child. Her husband has belonged for only three years. They are great friends with the pastor. He likes reading, and has just asked me for a Catholic Bible.

Motherhood: masses of beds in a tiny room – no room even to move among them. It must be horrible when all the babies are crying. On the next floor there are some charming rooms, but what do they cost? Aren't all mothers God's children? Is it only true for some of them that to give birth to a child is a wonderful mission? Are all the others just animals?

S., 6 October 1964

To his parents: The loudspeakers are really at it now – it's the feast of Santa Teresinha. We've got to put up with ten days of it. The church square is crowded with people – simple ordinary people, who love children, who gaze in wonder at the sideshows, who like to drink a little cachaça – in short who are going to forget for a few hours the sordid misery they'll go back to in the morning... For once I've no meeting on tonight. So I've just been for a stroll. I had a cup of coffee with a prostitute who was holding court – her form of communion. Later I chatted with a woman Adventist who complained that I hadn't been to see her for a long time. I bought a packet of cigarettes, and spent a few minutes with some of the lads. I then came back here to write this, but I think I'll go out again afterwards, for with the records blaring outside it's impossible to sleep. (Only Richard, with imperturbable calm, is determined to go to bed. He treats it as a matter of principle – I admire him!)

The fiesta began with mass – everyone joining in very well – and indeed there are crowds at mass every evening. The singing and fervour are progressing. This evening we have just installed a loudspeaker system in the church, and at last this one seems to work. We've been trying to get one put in for ages, but it's hard to find an efficient kind. The church is so big that it's most necessary.

I spent the day today with Pedro and the two full-time ACO workers. We had a useful time, going over everything together. The ACO is getting bigger and better.

A few days ago the Lord gave me a great privilege. I spent two days at a leprosarium on the other side of the island of S. You could hardly believe what it's like: absolutely medieval. The whole place is filled with a stale and nauseating smell of putrefying flesh. As they have no regular priest I've promised to go at least two days a month. People like lepers, prisoners, prostitutes and alcoholics really are the poorest of the poor. When I find the ACO work too hard, I know where I shall ask to be sent.

Before that visit, I thought there were no contemplatives in the district – which would mean that the Church here was incomplete; but I realize now that I was wrong. There are contemplatives here – men and women who have renounced everything, sacrificed everything. Their enclosure is leprosy, and many of them are leading a totally contemplative life.

Yesterday was a full day. In the morning I went to give first communion in the next parish, where I had partly prepared the children. I then went by boat, *la lancha*, with thirty men and girls to the old people's home at Ponte São Silvo: heard

117

confessions, said mass, gave communion in all the rooms of the home. We swam in the sea. We lunched – it was the multiplication of the loaves, with everyone sharing what they had with the rest. Then a procession (which they love). Back to the parish, dialogue mass, and finally an ACO meeting in another part of town. Not really an unusual programme here; and as I walked home I was able to make a long meditation in the soft warmth of the evening. My meditation was cut short a few yards from the church when I came upon two fellows fighting each other with knives. What a fantastic life!

The loudspeakers are still roaring away, and I can hardly think straight. Richard is going to bed. Yves is finishing his Office. Life is fine.

DIARY

There was a meeting today to elect the new officials for the neighbourhood community. Our ACO preparation team had members in each of the two opposing camps. It's very hard to unite respect for differences of commitment like this with unity in the faith. The priest's role? I can only thank the Lord for the attitude of Maria and of Sebastiao, and their help.

The MEB: major new decisions are being made after our meeting with Dom Poletta the other day.

A man fell down in the street, spitting blood. Tuberculosis. They called the Pronto Soccoro, the emergency service. When the ambulance got there the driver took one look at him and said, 'I'm not taking anyone with TB,' and left again.

A woman came from the interior to get treatment in town because there were no doctors where she lives. She went to one. He gave her some medicine and charged a high price for it. It said on the label: 'Free sample: not for sale,' but she couldn't read, so the doctor took the opportunity to make something out of her.

Blood: the doctor has an order entitling him to as much

blood as he needs, and he's had it for three weeks. One patient is still waiting for a transfusion. 'Whatever has he done with the blood? Sold it?'

S., 14 October 1964

LETTER

To his parents: I'd like you to know that this letter represents an interval inserted by force into a life of movement, activity, endless meetings, and here I am, happily withdrawn from the restlessness of our parish district. The only way of getting this written was to take refuge in the seminary, and in any case I'm starting a retreat tomorrow at the Vincentian college. Yves has just left us this morning in the *Teco-Teco*, the little two-seater plane that travels round the interior: he's going to spend three weeks' holiday at Viana.

The dry season has begun. It's terribly dusty, so you have to keep changing your shirt, but I love the heat; I've never once missed the snow or the cold.

At the moment, in the midst of all our other activity, we are trying to find some nuns to come and live here at Santa Teresinha. It would be a tremendous help: we could have a medical centre, catechism classes, a small school and kindergarten, dressmaking classes, courses in hygiene, cookery, etc. It would be a great step forward for the neighbourhood.

The ACO is making another attempt to start something that was cut short by the 'revolution' – to form an association for domestic servants. Theirs is one of the most humiliated and neglected of all jobs. But it'll take patience – they've got to become aware of themselves as people before they can form anything.

I enclose a photo of the three of us – we wouldn't win any beauty contest. But to give you an idea how under-developed the place is, I may tell you that no photographer wanted to take all three of us together: 'We never do that – we haven't the equipment for it'!

119

LETTER

To his former parishioners and friends: Greetings to every-one! ... I haven't written one of these letters since 15 June, and you're all wanting news... Here we go then, and this is especially for all those who have written to me and not had a reply... Heartfelt thanks to all who have sent their sympathy, and have offered to send material help... Without my asking for money, you have sent me seven hundred thousand francs! It's terrific, and will help us with a lot of things – emergency help, medicine and getting people into hospital, the 'youth centre' where the YCW are setting up a small training workshop, fitting up the dispensary for the Uniao dos Moradores (neighbourhood community), money to help the ACO take part in the next national conference at Recife, etc. We also want to get some nuns here, so we must start thinking about buying or renting a small house for them.

There are three of us here at Santa Teresinha now. To-morrow it will be four months exactly since Richard arrived, covered in dust, after a bone-shaking journey along muddy roads that are caving in everywhere. Richard is now chaplain at the São Vincente college, and is also working with the YCS. It was hard work at first, because he had to start almost from scratch. Yves remains parish priest, and I stay at my post as diocesan chaplain of the ACO... Before he left for the Council, Dom Marcelo also asked me to be chaplain to the university students, at least till January. They form a kind of senior YCS in the University, but with a heavier stress on commitment. The university complex at S. includes faculties of law, philosophy, medicine, pharmacology, social service and a nursing school.

At the first meeting, the departing chaplain, Padre Mesquita, now to be a parish priest in the interior, said to me, 'You'll find seven hundred new children suddenly brought into your family.' The university group has a small kernel of good leaders, but here too one has to start almost from scratch, for the university world here is extremely conformist, and recent events have aggravated this tendency. Nor is there any contact with the national leaders (though this is typical of our very isolated geographical situation).

I could tell you some fantastic stories if I had time. Here's one : Hermogenes, spitting blood and certainly dying of TB, had to stay in a miserable palm-leaf hut open to all the winds, and completely alone. Together we wrestled with doctors, hospitals, sanatoriums; there were X-rays and sputum-analyses, and so on. I went to the doctor five times to get him to go and see Hermogenes who couldn't even get out of his hammock. Five times the doctor answered, 'Yes, I'm coming.' The fifth time, I took a taxi, and we went and caught the doctor at dinner-time. 'He won't recover,' and he refused to have him in hospital. But I had sworn that Hermogenes shouldn't go back to his 'home' – his horrible hut in the mud with water coming in every high tide... All day I dragged the dying man round the streets of the town – at least it's better to die fighting. The doctor in charge of the sanatorium also refused him. He said, 'Look, we have ninety beds, and there are more than five thousand known TB cases in S.' We went to the sanatorium : I told the matron what the doctor had said, but I said, 'He simply can't go home... If you haven't a bed, surely he could have some kind of couch.' She agreed. I went to talk to the cook, and also explained the situation to the other patients... But I had scarcely left when they turned him out again. God knows how, but he dragged himself over to Santa Teresinha... The next day the neighbours said he was trying to kill himself. But we still fought on. The neighbours made a real chain of love around him; every day they visited him and took him all his meals. I nearly went mad looking for help in all directions, and managed to get his injections and tablets. It went on for four months. And now, we seem to have won. I don't know whether the cure is complete, but Hermogenes is a different man. He's looking for work. Everyone says it's a miracle – and they may be right: a miracle of love, when the poor work together to do something which seems hopeless...

Yet there are hundreds like Hermogenes all over Santa Teresinha, and thousands in S. There aren't enough hospitals or doctors. Only hospitals with an organization behind them (here the very imperfect Social Security) get anything like adequate material support. Most of the patients go hungry. The other day I was in a hospital at supper time: they had a glass of tea and a scrap of dry bread. There was some kind of soup too, but nearly everyone refused it, it was so revolting.

The hygiene is appalling – yet one can't blame the doctors; most of them are doing absolutely all they can, but they haven't enough equipment, or help, or money...

In our district, there are now two 'neighbourhood communities', each with a little *ambulatorio* (dispensary) and two doctors who examine people for nothing. The problem remains the medicines... The people haven't enough money to buy all the food they need, let alone anything extra... So many thanks to everyone who has sent us things, or is sending them.

Did I tell you that I now spend two days a month with the lepers? I've promised to go the first Thursday and Friday of every month. The leprosarium is opposite the town, three quarters of an hour by motorboat, in a village called Bomfim... There are more than five hundred lepers having treatment there, but alas, there remain thousands in the interior who get none. It is an amazing sight – a hideous one, which would be unbearable to any but the eyes of faith. Three Sisters of Charity live among them, and care for them with total dedication. I go from house to house and am getting to know them all; I hear confessions and take communion round. The souls inside these ruined bodies are often truly magnificent... There are some without ears, or noses, fingers gradually going, some without arms or legs, eyes destroyed, hideous swellings that appear, grow together, become encrusted, bleed and waste away... I've heard the same cries as I read in the psalms – 'Has the Lord forgotten me, is the Lord asleep? All night long I have cried to him... Lord, save me, I can stand no longer...'

I go from house to house, carrying a little stool, since the Sisters advise me to be careful where I sit. The hardest thing to face is the school, where the poor little leper children attend so closely to the teaching they receive from two masters who are lepers too.

I've also been to visit the new Baptist pastor. He is blind and can no longer walk. We spoke of Christ's love of the poor, and of the reunion of all Christians.

I shall never forget the sight of one woman who dragged herself to me for confession. Her body was just one huge wound... While making her confession, she suddenly noticed that her fingerless hand had begun to bleed... Furtively, partly from shame and partly to spare me such an unpleasant sight, she hid the bleeding hand... I then saw great tears falling from her eyes, as she wept in total silence. That was what struck me most – not that she cried, but that she cried so silently.

Yves, Richard and I were having an interesting discussion the other day – about the phenomenon of all the Protestant sects here in the north-east. Suddenly Yves said, 'You should write about it.' It's hard to write – much easier to explain in conversation. I was describing the meeting I had had with the two Adventist pastors (Assembleia de Deus), who had invited me to their home to convert me. It was interesting from an ecumenical point of view, but also a chance to understand something more about the psychology of hundreds and hundreds of our people... It seems to me that the success of the sects and the ease with which they make 'conversions' – even from among Catholics – are due to something very profound, something far deeper than the level of apologetics. That is the first thing one must understand about them.

It seems to me that most people here live in a completely Old Testament world: the mentality, the customs, the deepest responses of the people, even their social structures, suggest that they live in fear of a great God who is awesome, just and punishing, a God who has propounded a rigid law – and that the mass of the people have not yet received the revelation of the merciful God, the God of love, the God who is their Father. The cries I hear at the leprosarium are the cries of the Old Testament psalmist, the despairing cries of ardent but untutored faith. Another leper said to me exactly what the man born blind said to Christ (with an Old Testament attitude which Christ was to lead him far beyond): 'I must certainly have leprosy because of some sin I committed when I was young, though I can't remember what it was...' In effect it wasn't just the man born blind who was speaking, it was the voice of his times, and one can say the same of that leper...

Another example: in a country where there is in practice no administration of justice at all, people have to carry out their own justice; even in the towns the police are inefficient, and as for the 'interior' ... well. Everyone is armed, either with a revolver or a *façao* (knife), worn in the belt. It is clear that the people, because of the nature of their social structures, still live by the rule of 'an eye for an eye', and that their struggles of conscience will be restricted to the Mosaic law: 'Thou shalt not kill!' Christian charity, forgiving injuries — no one objects to it, but no one practises it (generally speaking, that is) because they haven't yet reached such a degree of advancement. Similarly, 'Thou shalt not steal' doesn't mean here quite what it means in a modern capitalist situation. They still live in a patriarchal society where what belongs to one belongs to all: as in the Old Testament, community values are very strong, but there is no understanding yet of the value of the individual. 'Thou shalt not steal' is interpreted something like this: 'What you don't need you have no right to take, nor to steal. But what you need you can take.' (Let it be said, by the way, that we have a lot to learn from them in this; we have so stressed the value of the individual, in a perspective falsified by middle-class selfishness, that we often in practice forget the values of the community...)

Something similar could be said about God's command to Moses: 'Thou shalt not covet they neighbour's wife.' As in Abraham's day, most of the men have several wives, either in succession, or, often, at once. In Moses's time, God tolerated this until they should learn better, 'because of the hardness of their hearts' – in other words, because they weren't yet ready to rise to a higher level. What should one think of these poor people? Who would dare cast the first stone of theoretical moralism? The other day I was talking to a woman in my neighbourhood: 'Do you live with a man?' 'Yes,' she said, 'three days a week, because the rest of the time he goes to Dacara (another district) where he has a wife and children'!! But she wasn't complaining. She was accepting the whole thing as quite natural. And 'natural' is just the word for it: here people live and think at the level of natural morality; they haven't yet got to the supernatural level. There are thousands of instances one could quote to show this... Here people are very 'human' – certainly far more so, in one sense, than we are in France. For instance the rules of etiquette are reduced to a minimum, so that people have no complexes and feel at home everywhere. They are very kind, and extremely tolerant; and their kindness is basically 'natural' because it comes from an instinct in the blood, a biologically healthy need for affection. It's an excellent base on which to build supernatural love, but only a base (one which we sometimes seem to have lost). Tolerance: yes, there is openness, receptiveness, acceptance ... but also acquiescence in all that fits in with the natural law, without any idea that one could or should reject what is contrary to the supernatural law...

Here's an example of what I mean: the other day I went to say mass and talk to the old people in the Home across the water. I took with me a group of young people and a few adults. One man from our district asked me whether I knew the young woman with him: yes, I knew her... He then began to explain to me that his wife had become insane a few years ago, and was put into a mental hospital, and that he couldn't possibly bring up his children alone... I was talking about his children (there are eight of them), when he interrupted me to say, 'And I need a woman, too. I can't live alone,' as if it were the most natural thing in the world. I tried to make him think about the value of being faithful to his real wife, who is still alive, but he smiled at me as if to say, 'You're not talking in human language at all; you'll never convince me...'

Yes, in the north-east, we live in the Old Testament, and I think that is the ultimate reason for the success of the sects, for the sects remain almost wholly at the level of pre-Christian revelation... I pointed this out to the Adventists the other day: 'You stress the importance of the foundations of the house (the Old Testament), and you are right ... but you have forgotten to build the house itself (the New Testament), and there you are mistaken. Jesus said, "I came not to destroy (the foundations), but to fulfil, to complete (the House)." '

It seems to me that the situation our people are in now – this mentality, these structures – must give us to think; we must look for a suitable catechesis, and the right pastoral methods. It puts things in a quite different light to see our people here as people of the time of Christ; half Old Testament Jew, and half pagan ... and to see in the few genuine 'faithful' the fervent and enthusiastic community of early apostolic times... The further I go myself, the more I feel myself to be living in the very circumstances of Jesus, in some part of Judaea or Samaria... At every corner of the street you meet a ragged beggar asking alms 'in the name of Jesus' '... and God will give it back, and reward you with happiness'. Everyone gives, and if they have only a large note, the beggar gives them change. That's how I picture the beggars in Christ's time.

As then, too, you meet lepers, and they cry out with the same anguish, the same burning faith. And, as then, your home is no more than a 'tabernacle', a tent, a fragile and impermanent shelter that sometimes collapses, so that you have to build another nearby... As then, people live close together, no one likes being alone. The love of processions explains and symbolizes very well that need to be together, that pleasure in being with others, in getting into a group, in forming a people ... just as the people followed Christ and clung to him... As in his time, you meet genuine sinners, sinners who make no secret of it. They don't commit the Cellophane-wrapped, 'aseptic' sins of our hypocritical western civilizations; these are crude, sturdy, strong, honest, visible sins : no one kills underhandedly – they kill bloodily, with knives or guns. The prostitutes display their charms openly, and everyone admits susceptibility ... yet alongside this there is great sensitivity, great straightforwardness, and a childlike spontaneity in the faith. As in Christ's time, the people live far closer to the 'mystery' – the mystery of life, of death and of love. They recognize their dependence on the weather, on sickness, on such things as the fire that destroyed five hundred houses in a quarter of an hour in the working-class district of 'Brasília' not long ago... As in Christ's time, epidemics can kill great numbers; and, as then, the children run to the priest when he goes down the street, and cling to him, for their age-old instinct tells them that he belongs to God (and we don't wear clerical clothes, any more than Jesus did).

Pray for me – pray for us all.

Part 4
Love is conquering now

LETTER

To his parents: I still remember what a dismal, foggy month November is, with a permanent drizzle of rain, at home...

Here, thank God, it is warm from six in the morning on. One has to keep bathing, and I wander about all day in a thin shirt. You say you are surprised that I don't complain of the heat, but that's the last thing I'd ever complain of – you really know you're alive in this sort of weather.

At the moment I'm alone. Yves has just left Viana for Recife, to take part in a YCW conference. And Richard has gone to Fortaleza, for a YCS conference. I've got my hands full, but Yves will be back by 5 or 6 November, and Richard a bit sooner.

Last Saturday there was a most interesting meeting involving various different movements; it was Catholic Action day. I said mass on our kitchen table, with everyone round it – a real family meal. After mass we had our coffee and bread 'in communion' round the same table. And there were no artificial flowers.

On Sunday, another splendid meeting – of nearly 150 girls who work as maids. The attempts the ACO made before the revolution are being taken up again (as I must have told you) to form an association for domestic servants, the first step on the way to a trade union. They are very responsive, and really want to do something together.

The time goes so fast there is certainly no chance of being bored, what with the parish, the ACO, and now the University group too. All goes well. I'll stop here, and wish I could send you a puff of our nice warm air to cheer you up. It's the pineapple season here and they're very cheap. The marvellous thing about the north-east is that we have fruit all the year round – your dreams come true, Father! The only black spot is that there isn't any rhubarb!

Two days with the lepers at Bomfim. God has recently woken in me a very intense response which I will try to analyse:

1. Seeing, discovering (believing, realizing as certain, becoming truly aware of) the presence of Christ in the person of other people – of the poorest, the most unimportant, the smallest, the most unattractive.

2. The suffering Christ. A call to move from a natural sympathy to a supernatural compassion (making up what is wanting to the sufferings of Christ).

3. Christ rising from the dead, and already risen. Praise, wonder, thankfulness in faith for Christ's action (despite all appearances) in transforming people towards newness of life. A new life of love – and there are some already living that life.

4. Christ is now speaking and calling, speaking to me and to us all, calling me and all of us to fight against material evil, to abandon self-interest, to put the kingdom of God first.

A boy died yesterday: his mother was mentally unstable, his father the poorest of the poor. Their house was continually flooded. I had managed to get him accepted in the children's ward because some prestige still attaches to the priest, but without such help the poor can get nowhere.

The prostitutes, there are so many. I visited one yesterday at the Santa Casa hospital. Her look of pleasure and excitement when I gave her a little catechism!

One woman, married the first time according to civil and religious ceremony; her husband walked out, apparently to the next state, and she thinks he committed a murder, but hasn't had any reliable news. She's now re-married, civilly, and tells me, 'My husband is a good Catholic, and wants to be married in church.'

I've just been on a sick-call to a man of sixty. He made a

good confession : his first. He also made his first communion. I talked to his children as well. His son had made his first communion, but not his daughter-in-law. The family come from a place in the country where there is no priest and the nearest church miles away. It's the sort of thing that keeps happening. A few days ago another sick man made his first confession and communion in just the same circumstances.

There is remarkable friendship and sense of community among the people in the sanatorium : when I told them of another TB sufferer I'd discovered in the district, they made a collection of pills – secretly, of course. I took him a whole parcel of them, three different kinds. There were two collections – one from the men downstairs, another from the women upstairs. They are so kind – and so tactful. They won't let me sit on their beds or touch their things – though personally, I don't worry at all. They are simply ready and waiting for the love of God.

One Catholic man has just been invited to join the freemasons.

I've now had two meetings with our maids' group. They're terrific. Most of them – nearly three quarters I'd say – come from the interior.

Today – 4 November 1964 – was my first full day working in the ACO centre. So many wonderful contacts. The Lord is good.

Leprosarium of Bomfim
6 November 1964

LETTER

To *his sister and brother-in-law*: For some reason I've been thinking back this evening to my interrogation by a lieutenant from the military barracks a few days after the *Golpe* in April; he was trying to prove that the MEB was subversive, i.e. communist. He showed me a paper he had found in the MEB offices with a photo of a starving peasant, his face

133

drawn with suffering and hunger. I thanked him, but assured him that as a priest in the district of Santa Teresinha I didn't need any photos; that my own eyes were a very accurate camera which took hundreds of snaps like that one every day: starving men, women and children; he might like to spend a few hours with me visiting the district and see for himself. I told him that though I was not myself a communist I found it deeply horrifying every time; if he wanted to know what subversion was, he had only to think about this kind of sense of horror: revulsion against hunger, against suffering, against a system which keeps men in the slavery of a condition unworthy of a son of God. 'Subversion' means turning the established order upside down, and it isn't communism that is doing it, but poverty and the structures of poverty; they *are* a reversal of right order, they frustrate God's plan of justice and love (for true order as envisaged in God's plan may well be very different from the established situation).

This evening, after a day and a half at the leprosarium, I've come back to this thought: 'If I weren't a Christian and a priest, I would be a communist.' It is frightful: these poor lepers have already lost absolutely everything – their families, their health, any kind of social life. Most of them know they'll never leave this place, and still worse, they are almost totally abandoned by the public authorities. You would be appalled to see the place. Private houses and communal houses all revoltingly dirty, leprosy (literally) on the walls, underclothes filthy and bloodstained, outer clothes in rags, food at starvation level. Yesterday and this evening I was there at suppertime. Yesterday, they had a few spoonfuls of *farofa* (cassava flour with no nutritive value whatsoever) and one glass of coffee; this evening one small dry roll and one glass of coffee – and that was *all*. They tell me that it's the same every evening. The only variation is sometimes three dry biscuits each (smaller than the kind we have) and one glass of coffee – there's not enough coffee to have more than one. It is all really desperate. And add to that the same conditions I see every day all over my district, in the hospitals, etc. – it makes a pretty frightful picture.

I must stop before my pen turns into a knife or a gun. The suffering of the poor cries to heaven for vengeance. I could weep. The sight of these poor ruined bodies is horrible : hands without fingers, arms without hands, legs without feet, eyes non-existent, ears gone, noses reduced to hideous excrescences. The eyes of faith make it possible to see beyond all this, though, and it is not really their physical state that is the intolerable thing. What is absolutely intolerable is the way they are despised and abandoned.

I'm sorry – I shouldn't pour out all this to you, but you happen to be with me tonight – I'm making use of an evening's peace to write this. Tomorrow morning I take the *lancha* (motor launch) back to S. And since I am writing, it's impossible not to talk about the thing that fills my mind.

I may say that the town itself is very attractive. As I went to say mass a little while ago I paused to admire the ocean pounding on the shore close by – what a contrast to the horror of the human situation here ! It is so beautiful as to be almost unbearable – the empty beach, the sunset reflected on the waves, the mysterious horizon of sea and sky, the delicious warmth of the north-east, the cocoa-palms swaying gently, and the stars twinkling in the sky like friends.

I can't help thinking about what happened this afternoon. I went into a women's ward to see the patients. They were very much surprised and thought I must have come to the wrong place; when I said, 'No, why should you think that?' they told me that no one ever goes to see them They have been told they are on the way to hell, they are damned, they are in the gutter, they are lost, etc. I suddenly got the message : they are prostitutes, and therefore lepers twice over. So I told them that Jesus loved them a great deal, and that I too loved them since I was his representative, that no one had any right to cast a stone at them, and that, honest man that I was, I should almost certainly be inferior to them in the kingdom of heaven; I added, 'Whenever I come to Bomfim in future, my first call will be to you.' They find their isolation extremely hard to bear – it's worse than the isolation of leprosy, because of the contempt that goes with it, a contempt condemned in the gospel. I love prostitutes because they are the poorest of the poor, and because they are so often so close to Christ. I don't always say this to everyone, because they wouldn't understand, but 'they' certainly heard it *con brio* in my sermon this evening.

There are still thousands of things I want to tell you, but I must leave some of it for May 1965 when I'll be with you for a while: that is, I hope to say it then, but probably I'll be unable to say anything at all – just, 'Has it been raining long?' or 'It's hot in the north-east, you know.' We shall see. In any case it'll still be the same me – a bit balder, just as stupid, sometimes quite quiet and sometimes very angry indeed, but, I certainly hope, affected by three years' extraordinary experience. My heart, my mind, my priesthood will never be the same again...

DIARY

Working-class solidarity: I met a fellow one night at the garage door; he was going to stay on duty all night in place of a mate who was ill, even though he'd already done a full day's work. Every night, all the workers in the garage are taking turns in replacing their sick mate on night duty.

There's a woman with leprosy in our district; the doctor at the leper-dispensary has refused to take her into the leprosarium.

Pedro is worried about the forthcoming union elections.

He's finding it hard with so many of this world's cares on his plate to keep his vision of the apostolate, and not neglect his diocesan A C O work.

The domestic servants' association is off to a flying start now. The Correia team began well with a study day last Sunday. We talked of the mystery of the cross that we must live: if the working class is to be saved, our A C O must enter that mystery. Growing pains are a proof of life, but that life must be the life of Christ. There's a São Vincente team, and one in Santa Teresinha. I must do a lot more praying if I am to link the lives of my people, and of my Christian workers, with the life of Our Lord.

Today I visited the *Terreiro* or 'Drum of Minas'. It's very strange... On the one hand there's a great reverence for the talents, the special qualities, the unique expressions of the soul of the people (their rhythms, dances, costumes, etc.); on the other there's paganism – women 'possessed by occult forces' who behave as if insane, yelling, and rolling on the floor like animals, hideously contorted. I said to them that:

1. We have the dignity of the children of God. We must work for happiness (and health, and so on) and above all we must look for God with the best that is in us: our minds, our wills, our hearts (and not just through the bizarre and peculiar).

2. We each have a *personal* destiny. Salvation, though involving the whole community, must be something personal: freedom, grace.

This *Terreiro* (the meeting-place of the *Macumba*) in the Rua 14 do Março, contained 102 women and four men (the men do the drum-beating). Each year they elect officers. They pay a small monthly subscription for membership, and then receive free assistance in time of sickness, operations and so on.

Ribamar, an A C O leader from the Correia. His wife has

died. They had faith in a woman healer who told them, 'A woman has cast a spell over her – there's nothing you can do.' So they did nothing: no doctor, no medicine, they simply let her die!...

Leprosarium
4 December 1964

LETTER

To his parents: I'm back among my beloved lepers. We're planning to organize a Christmas party for them – 'we' being *all* the people of Santa Teresinha, Catholics, Baptists, Adventists (I know a few Baptist and Adventist families quite well now). And a group of us came yesterday to visit Bomfim and have a preliminary meeting. Unfortunately Neide, an Adventist, became ill the previous night; she cried because she couldn't come with us. I'm sure that this is the way to unity, doing things together. I know in advance that I'll be criticized, but Jesus is here, present in the person of our poor and suffering brothers. He is calling us all together, and in doing so tells us to knock down all our barriers. Love always wants to knock down barriers, *all* barriers...

I got Mother's letter and it has almost completely reassured me as to her being well. I'll say 'Happy Christmas' early too, to be sure to say it in time.

This morning I 'went for a walk' with Christ among the poor ravaged bodies here, but I know that inside these bodies are hearts that give him great joy.

One woman explained that her illness was certainly a great grace as far as she was concerned. She talked to me while they were removing the bandages one after another from the bits of fingers she has left: 'If I'd been healthy I might perhaps have lost the one thing that matters, the love of God. Jesus knows what he is doing.' Another woman, a Protestant, now barely breathing, told me that her body was breaking up, but it is the spirit, the soul, that matters. She says that as her body falls away, she feels her soul rising to the Lord, being purified in love.

There seems little one can add to that, except to say a silent Amen. It is not that love *will* conquer; love is conquering *now*.

As you see, I don't get time to be bored here, what with one thing and another. Did I tell you about our last *romaria* at Riobamba? It was terrific. I must stop now, but it won't be long now before you see me again.

DIARY

Maria weighs barely more than seventy pounds; she's sick and weary. She has given her all to the movement, that the kingdom of God may come among the working class. She's preoccupied with problems – her family, her children, the future, house, rent, etc. – and doesn't eat enough (nor does Sebastiao, but then who does around here?). I practically had to use force to get her off to Ribamar for a month's holiday.

I thank the Lord for giving us the chance to meet saints like Maria. He 'uses' the poor to save the poor, and the means they use are poor too. I am grateful for being reminded of this.

The prostitutes at Bomfim – so near Christ and yet so far.

Our Christmas, with Catholics, Baptists, and the Assembleia de Deus. Our visit together. The generosity and openmindedness of Neide (Assembleia) and Helena (Baptist). The mystery of our disunity, and our longing for unity.

The nuns at Riobamba – they're a great group.

Today there was the election in the Weavers' and Spinners' Union. At this moment, half past midnight, they must know the results. Oh Lord, help Pedro and all the others to do what is best for your kingdom and the working class.

Antonio, one of the Fortaleza ACO: the problem of his wife and her favouritism towards the youngest children.

Bernard, who is nineteen, is in the advanced stages of leprosy. He arrived from the country four or five days ago, with his mother. A family in Rua de Correio took pity on them, but this evening they put Bernard out: 'We've got children, we can't keep you here.' We went together to Bomfim. If the nun hadn't taken him into the leprosarium we'd have had him in our house, but she did take him and he stayed there. What it is to be poor: a stray, with nowhere to go, no family, no friends, no home, nothing – just a patched shirt, and his hammock rolled up under his arm. In that situation, you do what anyone suggests, you accept any solution.

Leprosarium of Bomfim
2 January 1965

LETTER

To his parents and friends: At present there are only two of us at Santa Teresinha. Richard has gone to the next state for a short holiday. He writes: 'I hope you're not letting the hut get too untidy' – and it's true that Richard brings an element of order into the vagabond life Yves and I normally live. Yet Richard can do surprising things; in the same letter he says he has written to Brigitte Bardot to ask her to visit us! We had in fact jokingly talked of doing so. In case you didn't know, she is the idol of Brazil, and is at the moment staying near Rio. Of course she's only seeing one side of Brazil, and we thought it might do her good to see the other – the hunger and under-development and poverty.

A lot of people do visit us; two French priests each spent ten days with us on arriving in the north-east to work, and we're expecting a Brazilian seminarian. At present the house is full: a French engineer who has been in Brazil six years is here with his wife and three children. Anyone who wants to come, can... There is no substitute for actually being in a place; some things are just too hard to explain in any other way. It's impossible to take them in from a distance. For instance, our new archbishop has paid us several visits, and the last time he walked all over the district with us for a whole afternoon and evening. He's very simple and natural, and ordinary people find him easy to talk to.

How did you spend Christmas? Myself, I would echo the words of one of the ACO girls who came on our 'expedition': 'It was the most wonderful Christmas I've ever had...' We went to visit the lepers in Bomfim – four of us, people from this district and YCW and ACO members from all over town. We went from house to house, greeting people and making introductions, and after that we had a really extraordinary mass; it was a real community of love. I saw tears in many eyes, and I could hardly control my own emotion when the patients began one of their favourite hymns which expresses love for the world and a longing for beauty and love. One leper improvised an accompaniment on a simple flute made of bark – the music tore your heart out... At the end of mass, when we had sung the ACO hymn, we felt we had discovered the truth: *Que foi que a qui nos reuniu? Foi o Amor!* which means 'What has brought us together here? It was love!'

We then had a meal together, as we do on all our ACO study days, and those who had nothing to bring themselves got rather more than anyone else; we pooled everything, and simplified matters by not bothering with spoons or forks – just fingers. In the afternoon we had planned a little party in the dining-room, the largest room in the place, with singing, games, dancing, and presents for everyone. I joined in the dancing of course, and once again was made to sing 'Alouette', which seems to have become a tradition.

Yesterday, for the New Year, I went to say midnight mass for the lepers. Later we went across the sea in the other direction, to call on the old people's home. This time there were between seventy and eighty of us, and again that wonderful sense of brotherhood. The archbishop came too. An old lady of over seventy-five danced sambas and baions for us – she's a wonderful woman; they call her *a jardinheim* (the gardener). It was she, the last time I came out to say mass for the old people, who wanted to go to confession a second time – I think she was jealous when she saw everyone else going up to the priest!

Yesterday the archbishop said, 'I appoint you chaplain to the leprosarium until I can find someone permanent.' That's why I am here among my beloved lepers today. Tomorrow morning I shall say a very early mass so as to be on time for our ACO study morning in Piraï. In the afternoon there's to be another meeting, with the delegates who are to go to Recife soon for the ACO national conference. I then rush back for the six o'clock mass at Santa Teresinha, and later in the evening I have an ACO team meeting in the district of Nossa Senhora da Vitoria – but I can't stay till the end, because the *domesticas* (maids) have a party planned. It's really a party to help extend the association of domestic servants that they are organizing. Whew! When that's over I'll go home, probably on foot. I love my nightly walks – they do me a lot of good, and it's then that I get my thinking done. It's amazing what a lot there seems to be to think about at that time: all the people I've met and what they have said, all the sufferings and the joys I've come across, what my own reactions have been. Have I responded as a priest should? What would Christ have done? And precisely what is the Lord calling me to do in all this? Often when I get home in the evening after an ACO meeting like this, with my little notebook full of so many things and my heart even fuller, I meet some of the *crentes* coming out of their prayer-meetings with Bibles under their arms. And I think: that's right. God speaks in both books – the book of the Bible and the book of life. God speaks, he has spoken, he continues to speak every day. At first we don't understand him, or perhaps we begin by understanding the God who spoke in the past, but not the God who is speaking now, through the events and the people we meet. And as I walk through the warm night, I see the church of Santa Teresinha standing far off against the horizon, lit up, a symbol of the Church of the future that already shines for the eyes of faith, and which, despite the mess we've made of the present, still spurs us to enthusiasm. I'll go up the hill, and find Yves taking his shower; we'll chat together and have a cool drink. He'll tell me that the bricks haven't yet come, and that two benches have been stolen from the church, and that the YCW meeting was terrific. We'll say Compline together; then I'll have a shower, and we'll both go to our hammocks. Since I came to Brazil I've broken all my previous records – I'm asleep in between twenty and forty seconds! It's quite a life – and we certainly have no time to get bored.

In the parish, life goes on. I try to keep in contact with the people, and I go visiting as often as I can. If you're going to keep in contact, and try to enter into the concerns and ideas and sufferings of the people, and especially of the very poor, you simply must keep visiting. The other day I came upon an old woman who had leprosy (or so I assumed); I sent her to the leper dispensary, and they confirmed that she had. But despite the note I sent her with, they refused to take her in at Bomfim – 'No room', the familiar refrain... She was taken in by a kind neighbour, but the neighbour herself was very poor, and there were several young men and girls in the household... I went to see the director of the dispensary, but it was no use... I tried to have another talk with the doctor who visits the leprosarium regularly – a very nice man – who is horrified by the way the authorities simply abandon the lepers: 'We are more than ten million in debt... Our suppliers are refusing to give us food, one after another, because we can't pay... I don't know what we're going to do... It's humiliating... The state has found an effective cure for leprosy: no one dies of leprosy any longer because they die of hunger first. . .' Oddly enough, as I came back to town in the boat after one of my last visits to Bomfim, almost the same phrase kept going round in my head: 'No one dies of leprosy, they are all slowly dying of hunger.' One woman died quite recently, not of leprosy, but of inanition or anaemia.

But if I were once to start on the health problem, I could fill pages and pages – simply with dry facts. I could tell you, for instance, of Santana who has just died at the Santa Casa, after a struggle that lasted five months. When I first met her she was lying in her hammock, skeleton-thin, alive only through the generosity of her neighbours... Having visited her several times, the doctor agreed to operate for nothing if I could get her accepted at the Santa Casa (a hospital reserved in theory for the poor). Naturally they had no room for her. I returned to the charge again, and again, and again, till I finally heard myself saying: 'There's no room, but if you were to get 10,000 cruzeiros *vamos ver se naotem um jeito*' (which means: you'd try to find a way). So Santana got into the hospital. Before the operation, she needed blood transfusions. Since she had no money to buy blood, 'they' wanted to take some from her fifteen-year-old son, who's undernourished and not strong. Santana sent for me... In a situation like that, one feels a rising tide of anger that cannot be suppressed. What would you have done? I told them that blood isn't sold or bought; it's given. I gave some. Yves gave some. We called for volunteers in the neighbourhood. The *Verador* (something like the mayor of the district) gave me a note he got from the *Prefeito* which gave me the right to draw as much blood as Santana needed. Fool that I was, I passed it on to the doctor, and I never saw that letter again. You can see why people get to the point of wanting a revolution. There are priests who want to stir up revolution, but that's something that needs a lot of love, and I still feel pretty inadequate in the face of all these poor people. The day before she died, Santana wanted to go . . . I knew where. I think she was dreaming of a place where there would be love for all, a place where the poor would be loved. She has gone there. She was thirty-three – the age when Christ gave us his blood.

Oddly enough, it was just about that time that we three decided to stop taking 'mass-offerings'. . . Christ's blood isn't bought or sold either. Only people with money could ask for masses, and the masses were then 'theirs'. The people in our district are poor, and Christ's blood is like a mother's love : 'each has his share, and everyone has it all.' Now we say mass for one, two, three or four intentions, and anyone who wants to help us live puts whatever they want in the box. And in all logic, we have adopted the same attitude in regard to France : we pray for whoever we're asked to pray for, living or dead, and whoever wants to help us can.

Last month I was lucky enough to take part in a national meeting of university chaplains, near Rio de Janeiro. As it will probably be Richard who does this job in the future, he came along too. It was extremely interesting. We thought and spoke a great deal about being a priest. What exactly is a priest? What does it mean to be a priest in the world today? What does it mean to be a priest here in Brazil, here in an underdeveloped and developing country, here among the sub-proletariat of the north-east?

Perhaps the most important thing in Brazil – and all over the world – is training lay people, and helping them to become committed to the world as Christians. It is vital to draw people from the university world, because they are the leaders of the future, and, at least until the working class becomes aware of its own power, will have the greatest influence on the social, economic, political and cultural structures of coming years... But can we priests help them to become committed without feeling committed alongside them, without being in a sense equally committed? What matters is to work out the form of our commitment; above all it must not simply be a new and subtler kind of clericalism, a different way of seeking for prestige...*

In the pluralist world of today, Christians and priests must take their place in the building up of the world (a juster and more loving world) and in the building up of the kingdom of God; and while Christians have their place, so do the rest, *all* the rest, even if they are not aware of the fact... There are genuine values among non-Christians too, and as such they are supernatural values too, and already of use in the building up of the kingdom of God... Is our perspective wide enough

* Here is an extract from an article Paul Gallet had written a few months earlier, analysing the roles of the priest and the layman in relation to the two-fold task they face: evangelization and development:

'For us, Christ's priests, the choices are already made. We have staked all our hopes (and they are great) on a committed laity, but this has not in fact been our choice, but the direction marked out by the Church. It seems to me that this is the only *human* hope as well as the only way to evangelization: the two are as inseparable as soul and body. You cannot choose to save first souls and then bodies; nor on the other hand, can you say you will first work for revolution, and only then begin to evangelize. If we make people leaders, train them, support them, and get them to permeate the world around them like leaven, just what are we doing? What does it mean? Are we fighting physical poverty, or spiritual poverty?

'We priests are often tempted to intervene personally in order to give help where there is real physical suffering, and at times there is no alternative. But when we think about it afterwards, and realize that it can be no more than a stop-gap, we must not rest content with that kind of help, and the danger of paternalism that goes with it. ... No, we know that the situation can only be saved, and the revolution of justice take place, if there is a total change in structures, which means the involvement of laymen in greater and greater numbers and force, in all sectors of social life...

'We also know that it is only the improvement of the lot of the whole community that respects the dignity of the children of God... There is no respect for human dignity in giving the poor charity... And only through commitment (charity in action) will we extend the values of the gospel and build up the kingdom of God.'

146

to recognize them? Is our faith strong enough? Are our hands truly held out to our brothers?

Please pray for the ACO leaders. They are the great hope for the future of the workers (the same is true of the YCW too – sorry Yves!). And even in the present: here's an example. Jose Santos has just been elected president of the Uniao dos Moradores of Lira, the longest established neighbourhood community in S. A few years ago Jose Santos could neither read nor write, nor could he speak in public. He still lives in the same little beaten-earth hut, only a few feet from the mud and the incoming tide; but he has, thanks to the ACO, made enormous strides, and his neighbours elected him because they know him and see how he lives, and because they have observed all the improvements that have taken place in their neighbourhood which up till a few years ago was one of the poorest in the city... They know from experience that it has been the leaven of the gospel that has underlain those improvements. The rest was simple logic...

And Pedro – he's just been re-elected president of the Weavers' and Spinners' Union, one of the largest unions in the city; and that despite the fact that there was a really nasty campaign against him in the most classic demagogic style (a small-time politician from outside the trade altogether looking for popular support to get him the post of federal deputy; for him the union was just a springboard for higher things). But the workers know Pedro and have seen him at work; they reasserted their confidence in him with a large majority. Pedro was one of the first ACO leaders in S. and is at present a diocesan leader. Five or six years ago he couldn't read or write. His odyssey has been most interesting. When still quite young he became dissatisfied with the traditional Catholicism of rituals, processions and devotions that he'd been taught, and left the Church. He became a spiritist, and in his new faith found something he had missed in the 'folklore' Catholicism of his youth, a kind of mystique, a dynamism which was to help him to make the gospel a reality of his everyday life... With some difficulty he escaped from the toils of spiritism, but that of itself did not bring him to genuine Catholicism... There was still one more (providential) stage to go through – joining a spiritual confraternity in which he was helped to create a traditional but firm basis of Christian principles... Then came the day when he discovered an active Christian life through the ACO – that was a real revelation to him; he was as if lit up from the inside and his whole personality changed. To realize it you have only to see him, and hear him say : 'It wasn't me who came to the ACO, but the ACO that got into me.'

What a letter this is – you've certainly got your money's worth this time !

For some time now the electricity of Bomfim hasn't been working, and I'm typing madly away by candle-light... I've just finished my last cigarette, and there are large ants crawling over me (I'm stripped to the waist – it's more comfortable). I'm thinking about the lepers sleeping close by who will consume Christ's body in the morning... And how we are all more or less eaten away by the leprosy of selfishness, callousness, smugness or despair... And how the host is so tiny and the Body of Christ so vast... And how we too are so very small, and yet in spite of ourselves, there is something growing inside us... No, that's wrong, not something, but *someone* growing within us despite our limitations...

Outside the wind is blowing, a warm soft wind, I hear the fresh friendly swishing of the coconut palms. Jesus is born, and that is the secret of life; I know that he is being born somewhere now, in some part of the world... I pray that it may be in me.

Yves and Richard join me in wishing you all a Happy New Year. Please keep writing, and forgive us if we don't answer every letter. Our thanks to all the friends who are helping us, materially and spiritually. Thanks for your friendship too, all of you in la Minotière, la Bastelle, and Chesne-les-Monts, everyone in the ALM * and everyone else.

Recife
1 February 1965

LETTER

To *his parents:* The ACO conference ended yesterday. It was very interesting, with seventy or eighty delegates from all over Brazil, from the extreme north of Amazonia, to the south along the Argentinian and Chilean borders. There were fifteen chaplains, Canadians, Italians, Germans, Brazilians, and French (the largest group). I think we got a lot out of it, and the whole movement has become more aware of its responsibility, and generally stronger and more apostolic.

At present (following the *Golpe*) Catholic Action is having a difficult time. In some places it can cost you your life. The leaders from S. state are going back this morning – some via João Pessoa (where they are to get in touch with a maids' group), the others direct; and Pedro is flying, because he must be back at his job in the union. I myself shall leave after the chaplains' meeting ends, which will be on Wednesday morning. I shall certainly make a detour to C. to see Dom Poletta; I've not been able to get there since his enthronement, though he's asked me several times.

We came to Recife in crowded buses – it took four days. We left at between three and four o'clock in the morning, and travelled till ten or ten thirty in the evening; I don't think that throughout the journey we had more than fifty or sixty miles of made-up road. I need only tell you that the rest were like dirt roads at home, full of potholes and terribly dusty.

---

* ALM: Auxiliares Laïques Missionaires, a lay society whose members are trained in some of the more indispensable professions – e.g. as doctors, nurses, teachers – for working in cooperation with religious on the missionfield.

When we stopped at night we were covered from head to foot in greyish-red dust. The best thing is to shower thoroughly at night and then put the same clothes on the next day.

You would hardly believe how incredibly makeshift everything is here. One night, for instance, the headlights gave out at about ten. So, for the last forty-odd miles, a boy held his arm out of the window holding a small torch to see by ! That'll give you some idea.

No one here dies of heart failure (I have in fact never heard the word), because there's always a way round everything : *dar um jeito*.

On Monday evening, after the first day of the chaplains' meeting, there were thirty-five of us; several priests came from Recife and round about to augment the fifteen of us who took part in the national conference. It was very good : one felt a preoccupation with the situation of the very poor, and a sense of anguish over what the Church ought to be doing about it. Something is stirring... With us there is one full-time ACO worker, a Swiss, Jean Queloz, a terrific fellow. There is also Fr Faureau, chaplain of the world movement of Christian workers (MMTC) which coordinates all the workers' groups from all over the world. He arrived from France to take part in our conference, and is going on to Uruguay for the international meeting of the MMTC.

Our masses during the conference were tremendous; one had a real sense of renewal, and especially of community. This evening we have just been concelebrating with ordinary bread.

A new national committee has been elected. I was appointed to represent northern Brazil (after a meeting that ended at three in the morning !). The conference has provided a chance to make a lot of new friends, both priests and lay people.

Obviously I've not had news of you all this time, but I expect there'll be a bundle of letters when I get home. Oh yes, I saw Fr Joseph Lebon, who gave me loads of cigarettes. Many thanks! Joseph also gave me news of you – I gather he called while Mother was doing the washing! How are you all? How's your health, Mother?

My greetings to everyone. I positively *must* go to bed.

C., 11 *February* 1965

LETTER

To his parents: How I wish I could send you some of our lovely heat. It's eleven at night and I'm stripped to the waist and still sweating. In the daytime it was 94–95 in the shade – glorious. I got to Dom Poletta eight days ago, and it was a joy for us both. We're real friends. As C. is 'almost' on the way back to S., I have stopped by to see him. No sooner had I got there than he coopted me into four days of study with the (twenty-two) nuns of his diocese. It is a new diocese, only just created, and Dom Poletta is having a hell of a time getting anything organized at all. He has a sum total of twelve priests, almost no money, vast distances to cover with practically no roads, and as yet no active lay movements of any kind. Yesterday, the study days being over, we spent a day relaxing in the country, in a *fazenda* (farming property) called 'The Desert'. It was a wonderful day; Irismar, another priest, a great fellow, and I had long and frank talks about our work and life. We bathed in an *acude* (a rain-water hole), and were happily *not* attacked by the *piranhas* (greedy little fish who nibble perseveringly away at you till they've eaten the lot). As there wasn't a bus till the end of the week, some young people from C. offered to take me to Teresinha by air – the plane should have left C. early this morning, but developed some kind of fault, so now, all being well, I should leave tomorrow. It's no use being in a hurry in Brazil! This evening Dom Poletta interviewed me on the local radio for forty minutes. He asked a lot of questions – why I'd come to

Brazil, the ACO, our work in S., and the terrible poverty there. I asked whether I could say what I liked without its getting him into trouble. He replied that the truth must be shouted from the housetops, so I seized the opportunity. The broadcast was a bit subversive, but, after all, poverty and injustice are subversive too; it is they that overturn the order willed by God – not those who revolt against the 'established disorder'.

The state we are in is very different from S.; here there is a permanent drought. In France we say, 'Will it be fine tomorrow?' Here (now, in what should be winter) we ask, 'Will it rain tomorrow?'

There is great poverty in the countryside. The cattle are all bones, and the people are starving. Every day crowds, spurred on by want, pour into the town to look for work and something to eat. They are seriously considering a 'hunger march' of starving peasants who, rather than simply die, will come and loot the shops in C. Dom Poletta is very anxious indeed, and he's already warned the authorities.

The day before yesterday a priest was wanted for a sick-call. I went. It was about eighteen miles each way by jeep, along impossible tracks, through a desolate landscape : everything green had died under the scorching sun, as dead as things are at home in mid winter – not a leaf, not a blade of grass, just twisted tree-trunks and dried roots that look as if they're reaching up to catch a drop of rain from the sky. I stayed to dinner with the *fazendeiro* (the landowner). The agricultural problem is terribly complicated. This *fazendeiro* owns several *fazendas*, and this particular one is 'only' about seventeen and a half thousand acres ! But it's not his fault – it's the fault of a hopeless system. We need a good revolution, a real one, and with it a good five-year plan, and a whole lot of technology.

We three had a good team meeting today, for which I thank the Lord.

The day before yesterday Christ spoke to us once again through a parable (when one has reached a level of full illumination, he speaks clearly; but when one is still in a stage of preparation, he speaks in parables, i.e. through life). A mason found himself out of work; the man who had commissioned him to build a house had run out of money for the job. The mason spent a sleepless night worrying; the next day there was no more food for his wife and eight children. He went to the São Paulo market to see if he could find a friend to lend or give him some money for food, but he met no one. Then he saw a goat tied to a post, and he did something he would never normally have done: he untied the rope and 'stole' the goat, which he brought to Santa Teresinha to sell. The police arrived; they took him to the police station, but he took his eight kids with him and explained the whole thing. The chief of police declared: 'I can't put him in prison.' The people who saw what happened and heard the story quickly made a collection. So the man went home with his eight children, some money in his pocket, and a little hope in his heart...

Our neighbours. Their two daughters ran off several months ago, on St John's night, each with a boy. There were harsh words between the families concerned. Now both girls have been abandoned, and both are pregnant. They have come home to their parents. No money, no material help, no *apparent* suffering. The whole family is moving. They're going to an even more wretched house out in the mud, in 'Brasília', just to get away from any more rows with the boys' families.

At the ACO conference I heard this dialogue between two members, one from Rio Grande Do Sul and one from S.: 'What does milk cost in S.?' 'I don't know.' 'How do you mean, you don't know?' – and the member from S. replied, 'Well, I never buy milk; in my neighbourhood and all the poor districts of S. no one buys milk – no one sells it either. It's too expensive.' No wonder nearly sixty-five per cent of babies in S. die before they are a year old!

S., 1 March 1965

LETTER

To his family: For the past two days S. has changed completely – it's the Mardi Gras. S. is said to be the third best town when it comes to carnivals, and I can well believe it. The streets are exploding with gaiety. The Carnival here is basically a phenomenon *of the people*: for four days they forget hunger, joblessness, poverty. In the streets (and everyone is out in the streets) you see nothing but masks, costumes, singing and dancing groups, *blocos* (groups in fancy dress), parading through the town, day and night, with the hypnotic rhythm of a child-like people harking back to their African roots. They beat drums, saucepans, jam tins, bottles. Just now, in João Lisboa Square (in the town centre) I saw several masked figures making the sign of the cross in front of a church as they danced past – one of them was a man dressed as a woman, with a very sexy bosom...!

Brazil really is an extraordinary country. Even the lepers, whom I went to see yesterday and the day before, have organized a big dance. The thing we Europeans find hardest to put up with is the noise. For instance, all the year round there are four loud-speakers stuck up at a height of thirty feet or more pouring a flood of music down into our district of Santa Teresinha, the same music, from morning to night. It can start at five thirty in the morning – if someone has a birthday – and go on till eleven at night; and very often the *Macumba* spirit drums will then take over and go on all night long. At first you think it'll drive you mad, but you get used to it after a bit. The Brazilians love noise; they love anything that helps them feel less alone.

2 *March.* Whew – today's the last day of Mardi Gras. Tomorrow may be a bit quieter. Last night we went to supper with João and Annick (he's a Brazilian, she's French), and met a Chilean engineer and his fiancée, a local girl. We got home at one in the morning after an impassioned discussion on under-development, communism and the Church.

Did I tell you that our nuns have arrived? There are four – they're from the next state. The Brazilians immediately commented favourably on that – they're Brazilians. Whatever happens we mustn't remain a French group of spiritual colonialists. They are living in a wretched little house without running water (only a well) and no electricity as yet. We bought the house and have completely done it up for them. They wear ordinary clothes, and they are very friendly and easy to get on with. When we are at Santa Teresinha for meals, we eat with them, which works well.

DIARY

A woman from the Macauba district; her husband is most neurotic, and for twenty years now she's been really persecuted by him, and kept almost entirely in the house. He won't let her go out. It has got much worse in the last two years; he is continually talking of killing her, and keeps a revolver hidden in a drawer, 'so as to be ready', he says. She lives in perpetual fear.

A frank discussion with Silvio and Regina about their difficulties in getting on together. Our criticisms of one another may be reasonable (because of real faults) or quite unreasonable (because of differences in temperament which one must respect). What is needed is 1, the psychology to know how, and when, to speak; and 2, a willingness to accept differences – in other words, unselfishness.

155

It was Silvio who said to me, 'Padre Paolo! You, Padre, do a lot to help me, but the one who really does it is him [Christ].'

The wax objects offered to our Lady at Ribamar – and here at Santa Teresinha. When someone is ill, they bring to the altar a wax model of the affected part – an arm, a leg, a head, etc. Is this simple faith? Lack of Christian education? Superstition? Fanaticism? A stage in formation that one should respect?

The lads in the district who are homosexuals.

Maria Aranha, ACO leader from Lira: 'No, it isn't my friendship for Regina that has kept me in the *Uniao* (neighbourhood community) in spite of all the misunderstandings and troubles I've had there. It's Christ. If it hadn't been for him, if he hadn't been there, I'd have packed it in long ago.'

Police Lieutenant Santos: 'What is hard isn't just giving, but giving yourself. For instance, the other day, when I was on a job in the interior, I had a return ticket to S., but I stayed there and lost some time in order to help my brother who needed me.'

Today I went to visit a priest who left the priesthood thirty or forty years ago. He's *my* brother.

Today, just as I was leaving Bomfim, there was an uproar. There's an official at the leprosarium who has a wife and three children here in town, and another wife at Bomfim with a child. He arrived on the boat with a chicken he had just stolen from the second wife. She waded into the water after the boat with a huge club – and he brought out a knife. I don't know how they managed to avoid bloodshed.

A visit to the sanatorium, after a study day with the ACO leaders. Wherever I turn I find goodness. Thanks be to God.

LETTER

To *his parents:* I got to the leprosarium yesterday evening and I'm leaving in the early afternoon (normally I come every Sunday, either morning or evening, to say mass and visit the patients, and once during the week when I can – though this depends on my work with the ACO, in the parish etc.). Last night someone died – quite a good friend of mine. But what a dog's life they have. Fingers and feet are eaten away and then fall off. It begins with a sore and a lot of pain and a temperature; then they feel better and there's less pain, and it falls off. Modern medicine can do a lot, but it all depends on the type of leprosy, and how far it has got. And on top of everything else, we're in the north-east where people don't get any help anyway, and people without leprosy die of hunger...

The other day they operated on one – his fingers were removed; he lost a great deal of blood and had to remain almost without food until the following midday (the menu then : black coffee with a little cassava flour). Perhaps one day we might cross the water and try to get into the Governor's palace, with all these limping, crippled, dying people : we'd be thrown out of course, but at least people would hear about it.

Today 12 March, I'm concluding this letter. No news from France for a fortnight. I'm just leaving the ACO centre where we've been preparing for a study day in two days' time.

To make the church a bit less ugly we're going to plant coconut palms, flamboyants, almond trees, etc.

How are you all?

I must stop – I have no more time.

LETTER

To his parents: The rain has been coming down in buckets
since this morning, so I can't do much else but write. I shall
certainly try to write from Bomfim in future, because it
really is far quieter here. I'm in the residence of the *capelao*
(chaplain), and through the door which is open to the rain, I
can see the great palm trees silently weeping (also some socks
hung out to dry).

I left Santa Teresinha this morning about six thirty,
walked through the district, and then took the *kombi* to the
little harbour. On the boat a woman shared her umbrella
with me. I conducted a short hymn-practice, said mass,
preached (splendidly of course), baptized and got some coffee
from the Sisters. I've now got a short break; it is pelting with
rain. I'm about to have lunch, and then I'll go back into
town. I'll take the tram (a real historic relic that clanks along)
to the ACO centre where we are to have a conference of the
leaders' group, then back to Santa Teresinha by the Estrada
Nova (the new road) where I shall say mass and preach; after
that I go to the district of Nossa Senhora da Vitoria, where
I shall take part in an ACO team meeting; I'll go joyfully home gazing at the stars, if there are any, and listening
to the toads croaking in the mud. (It's my meditation time –
my head and heart are always full to bursting at that time of
the day.)

DIARY

Neide and the Santa Amelia factory. Some workwomen refused, but others agreed to sign the pay slip – a receipt which
stated : 'I have received such and such a sum of money for
holiday pay, etc.' They signed before receiving the money,
and never actually got it. The same thing happened over

158

the 'thirteenth month' pay which must be given by law in all factories. Neide went with another woman to claim it from the manager. He was bewailing the many difficulties the factory faces: 'We don't make enough money, we have too many outgoings, pay too much tax, etc. etc.' and he added, 'I may have to close the factory before long' – and there is already too little work to be had in S. Neide and some of the other women know – at least they are almost certain – that there's someone in the factory smuggling out cotton thread, and others helping her. One of the women knows someone in the police, and is going to get it investigated, after which... What next?

A retreat with the MEB girls, social workers and girls who teach catechism. Blessed are the poor in spirit...

The ACO retreat in Holy Week; thirty-five people came; thanks be to God.

The book question in schools at the beginning of term. There are two elements:

1. The difficulty of buying such expensive books for working-class families; is it possible to form cooperatives for buying and lending them out (this could be done through the neighbourhood communities individually or in groups)? It's a problem of structures and of people's approach.

2. Another more political problem is the constant changing of books used... This happens almost every year owing, they say, to changes in method, etc. There have been commissions to the Prefect and the Governor, and petitions to the President of the Republic. All this came up at the last ACO meeting at Santa Teresinha, and also at the Lire (all the problems and all the arguments thoroughly gone into).

There is a marvellous atmosphere of friendship and mutual acceptance between the two full-time workers.

The subject Raymonde brought up (had the courage to bring up!) at the São Vincente team study session: it began with the sermon given the other day at the cathedral 'to give thanks for the revolution (of April 1964) which has miraculously saved us from communism' – what rubbish! People's reactions were quite unequivocal. I quote:

'What a revolution – a complete failure!'

'We want no part of it.'

'It was a revolution of hunger.'

'Revolution indeed! There wasn't any revolution, and you can't commemorate something that hasn't happened!'

'Here in S. the revolution passed over us like a jet plane – right over our heads: it had no time to stop here, and we haven't seen any results from it yet!'

The government has sent a large sum of money to the railmen to finance a party: they've bought more than thirty cases of beer. Fewer than thirty people bothered to go to the official affair (radio-controlled by the army) celebrating the revolution.

The response of the dockers' union: during the official ceremony to commemorate the revolution, the army delegate spoke in praise of the revolution and then asked the workers to speak. Total silence. Suddenly an old docker, respected by all his mates, rose: 'This revolution,' he said, 'is no concern of mine, indeed no concern of the working class at all; but I should like to take this opportunity to make an appeal to the authorities, who are for once present, to warn them and draw their attention to the terrible poverty people are living in today. They can't take much more. It can't go on like this; things must change.' Nowadays the whole of the working class feels like this and says this kind of thing. When you think what people have heard in some churches, it's appalling! The revolution began with a rosary in its hands, and goes on with the mass. It's nauseating.

Fatima – a spiritist who has just given up spiritism. At the moment she's considering returning to the Catholic Church: 'Why did I leave the Catholic Church and go in for spiritism? I felt sick at the sight of priests in their cassocks –

everyone was afraid of them. But now that new priests have come, plain ordinary people, no one is frightened any more. They aren't any different from us.'

S., 9 April 1965

LETTER

To *his parents:* ... The other day at Bomfim a leper knocked on my door. He knew I was going to be away for some time in France; he asked me to thank my parents because they must have helped me to become a priest. He said, 'I must tell you this: before you came I dragged along without any hope. Now it feels as though I've begun a new life. You've helped me to make the whole thing different.'

I blush to tell you this; but there are some days when all the pain and suffering in the world bursts out into tears of joy. Joy is a tremendous force in a priest's life.

Here I stop, to fling myself into my hammock. I can't go on any longer today but I send you all my love.

Part 5
The poor have taught us the gospel

Back in his diocese in France, Paul spent some time on holiday with his family, and took the opportunity to get in touch with the French ACO, to renew links with most of his old friends and to make some new ones.

Here are some extracts from a conversation he had with a Catholic lay leader to whom he tried to give a good general picture of the situation in Brazil:

After three years in Brazil, you're home for a bit: it must be something of a shock to be back after only a few hours in a plane. What are your main impressions?

Well, here's one of them:

I timed my return to coincide with the Catholic Action Congress in Paris. I met a thousand leaders there. The only congress I'd been to in Recife was made up of seventy or eighty – representing the whole of Brazil! Numbers apart, the apostolic and human situations are tremendously different: here you feel the lay movement as something established, its leaders totally committed; there the leaders are still on the way towards a less advanced position than yours. Here I hear workers talking of working hours and structural reforms; there, it's a question of finding work at all, and earning enough money to stay alive.

Do you see any sign in Brazil that ignorance and poverty will be defeated by faith and charity in Christ?

One can hope great things of a people who hunger for God, and the Brazilians are deeply religious.

As far as evangelizing the Catholics goes, we have made a change: rather than constantly fighting against their folk-lore and all that goes with it we are trying to establish more and more links between the gospel and their ordinary life. Are they unhappy? Then that is a reason to cooperate: 'mothers' clubs' are being formed in which they help one another (sewing, cooking, child care...). Do they see how poor other people are? Then that is an invitation to join 'neighbourhood communities' and become the leaven in the lump, to develop their missionary concern. These neighbourhood communities have just formed a 'Federation' for the whole city of S. Recently the Federation elected a committee: ACO members form a large part of it, and there is one in particular who was attracted to communism a few years back, but has now, thanks to the ACO, begun to understand all the values of Catholicism.

I must explain that when we are thinking of the most pressing needs of the Church in Brazil, three stand out: the training of leaders, adult catechism classes, and vocations to the priesthood. Obviously, the first of the three will involve the other two: it is through lay people that we shall manage to adapt to the right outlook for evangelizing the masses; it will be in established Christian families that vocations to the priesthood and religious life will be found.

I'm not talking of pastoral attitudes that may be adopted here or there in a country seventeen times the size of France. We know of agricultural experiments the bishops are making in the north-east: faced with a degree of poverty unknown in Europe, priests and bishops are responding to urgent needs, simply out of charity, and with no wish to dominate anyone. But nothing is perfect, and there are people of some education who feel suspicious of the Church's attempts to help in these cases, people to whom such help seems to smack of the Middle Ages. It isn't that these people are anti-clericals (apart from a few who are influenced by communism or some other philosophy – there are those who talk a lot about something that seems to us here very old-fashioned: the positivism of Auguste Comte!) but rather that they object to the Church interfering in temporal affairs. But one certainly finds in the student world young people full of generosity who have a far deeper vision of the Church, for instance the leaders of the university Catholic groups, and of the MEB.

People sometimes talk to me of the great danger of communism; I prefer to talk of the great opportunities open to Catholicism. There must be a revolution of the gospel wrought by the young people and adults who are becoming leaders, and by a whole people who are spontaneously generous and religious despite not yet being evangelized in the full sense of the word. That at least is my long-term hope. Meanwhile ... we welcome anyone who wants to help – priests, nuns, lay people. One of our leaders, Raymonde, has come from Belgium. Fr Talvas lets the girls from the 'Nest' come to live among us. A group of lay auxiliaries are working in the interior of our state. The Council has encouraged the whole missionary movement which is taking shape out there, and which is vitally necessary until such time as Brazil becomes the living people of God, able to announce the gospel to their less fortunate brothers elsewhere.

S., 24 September 1965

LETTER

To his parents and friends: Back again in my beloved Brazil, I want to write at once to all of you whom I had the joy of meeting, and who showed me so much kindness, during my leave. First of all, a tremendous thank you to everyone for your friendliness, your interest in our work, and the material help you have so generously offered. Altogether you sent me back feeling stronger and with greatly renewed enthusiasm.

'It's not just one priest who is going, but through him the whole Church which is taking up the burden of material and spiritual poverty borne by our brothers in Latin America.' I was struck by how much this feeling has grown in France in the past few years.

These few months' break have done me great good: rest, family life, so many contacts, spiritual reinforcement, time for thought. I got into the plane at Orly on 3 September.

Yves (also on leave at the moment) came with me to the airport and saw me go, not without a tinge of jealousy, with which I entirely sympathized... Paris, Madrid, Rio de Janeiro...

On 4 September, at one thirty, we touched down – but as you know there is four hours' difference, so in Rio it was only half past nine in the morning. It was wonderful to be back in Brazil, with all the colour, all the humanity, the spontaneity, the kindness ... I felt as though I hadn't been away at all.

By two o'clock I was back in the midst of 'reality', with members of the ACO national team, drawn from almost all the states in the land. This annual meeting went on till eight. François (our 'coordinator' in Latin America, who has just spent a month with Richard, at present on his own in Santa Teresinha) came to bring me the latest news from the northeast.

After a brief visit to a young couple who have recently left S. to settle in Vitoria, and a call on four French priests at present doing their course in Petrópolis, I got on another plane on Sunday 12 September. When I began to see the good earth of S. below me, my heart started to thump; and when I got a bird's eye view of the mass of friends waiting to meet me I could hardly control my emotion... A woman sitting beside me asked, 'What's the matter? Are you sick? Have you a headache?' and I could only say, 'No, it's not my head, it's my heart'... When I finally set foot on the ground everyone went mad; they began singing 'Alleluia Paolo', and they rushed at me, everyone wanting to see me, touch me, talk to me, hug me.

Then at Santa Teresinha, the same thing again : I was assaulted by a gaggle of children who shouted and clung to me. I had to go through a packed church with everyone clapping; their singing made the poor church shake – and my heart too.

After mass we went to the ACO centre, where there was a

little outdoor party in honour of my return and Richard's birthday (he'd taken over for me with the ACO while I was away).

... So here we are. I'm settled back here again. The day after I got back, before I'd even had time to unpack, a woman came begging me to see her son of eighteen, a leper, and try to get him taken into the leprosarium.

At Santa Teresinha I can't go a hundred yards down the road without someone greeting me vociferously 'Padre Paolo, vem ça' (come here), or: 'So de longe? O senhor naö fala mais com os pobres?' (Do you only talk to us from a distance? Don't you talk to the poor any more?) And I have to go up to them and chat through the window, or go into the house: 'You're fatter,' or 'You're thinner'... 'How are your family?' 'Were they pleased to see you?' ... 'We thought you were never coming back, but you'll stay now, won't you?' When I got to the salina I had a sad bit of news: Hermogenes, the young consumptive I told you about, died two or three weeks ago. They tried to save him, but the Lord called him to himself...

We're in the midst of an electoral campaign at present. The election will actually take place on Sunday next, 3 October, for the new state governor. Everywhere there are banners, posters, notices, speeches... Yesterday evening, for instance, one of the loudspeakers in our district was bellowing till half past midnight, but I couldn't tell you whether it was in support of the present Governor or his opponent! (The same sort of thing was happening in Rio when I was there – they too were electing a governor; one evening the Governor in office spoke on TV from ten o'clock at night till eight in the morning without a break!) All the candidates vow to work for the Common Good – but what connection do such phrases have with the lives of ordinary people? One thing certain is that the situation of the poor is worse than it has ever been: two of the major textile factories have closed down (some time ago), and the spectre of starvation hovers over many working families.

The other day a young couple arrived, God knows how, from the interior, with two tiny children; all four were ill, starving, feverish and without a penny. The nuns took them in and fed them, and they are there 'for the present'. The husband has found a bit of work for a few days. Several young men have come to ask me to find them work. It's a terrible problem.

One interesting new phenomenon, in regard to the elections – something quite new in S., that hasn't been there in previous elections, is the existence of the many Uniaos dos Moradores (neighbourhood communities). These are a popular force with which, whether they like it or not, those who are elected now will have to reckon.

A possible hope for the future: apparently one of the richest petroleum deposits in the world has been found in our state. When I arrived from Rio all the newspapers were talking about it. Is it true? It could be the starting-point for economic development and a rise in the standard of living which is now so appallingly low.

Since Richard got here, the YCS has made great strides. The ACO is also continuing to grow in strength and numbers. New base teams are being formed. The two full-time workers are both doing wonders, but of course the ACO here is on nothing like the scale it is in France – as I realized when I went to the national conference at Issy-les-Moulineaux! Here we really have 'the Church of the poor', as Fr Talvas saw when he came through here on his tour for the 'Nest'... We are forced to work with the poorest of human means. But often the poor are very close to the gospel, and I can tell you that as I walk home in the evening after a group meeting – in between avoiding the potholes into which I still sometimes stumble! – I am quite dazed by the qualities to be found in these people, illiterate, without money, without food, living in their rickety huts surrounded by mud... For instance, can you imagine any priest in France asking the question I asked a girl from our district whom I met on the bus the other day: 'Has your house collapsed yet?' To which she replied, as if it were the most natural question in the world, 'No, not yet, but it won't be long now.' I'd passed down her street the previous day, and had a chat with her mother, who showed me her 'home': 'Look, it's going to come down soon; last night I heard creakings, and I had to get up and collect my belongings and go next door for safety.'

I'd like to give you something Brazilian in conclusion, and the best thing seems a short sentence I put down in my diary a couple of days ago. An ACO leader said it, while we were meditating the gospel together: A Esperança, a ultima que morre, 'Hope is the last thing to die'... It never dies, in fact!

S., 16 November 1965

LETTER

To his parents and friends: Since the mail is so dreadfully slow, I'll begin by wishing you all a happy Christmas. My thanks to all who have written, and I can only say how sorry I am not to have the time (or the peace and quiet) to reply to every single one... That is why I'm making a big effort to get this communal letter written today – I've shut myself up in the seminary to do it, because it's very hard to write or do any serious work at Santa Teresinha; it's fantastically noisy, with loudspeakers pouring out a non-stop flood of music that really gets you down after a while. The day before yesterday was the ladainha of Santo Lazaro, a traditional 'saint's' day when the people hold their own celebration in fulfilment of a 'promise'. In the afternoon, they got together all the dogs of the area and offered them a 'banquet' of many different dishes of food laid out on the ground. What a horrible custom in a place where *people* are dying of hunger! They then went through the neighbourhood singing hymns, and came finally with their 'saint' to mass ... before gathering for an all-night party... What price evangelization?

There are things one simply cannot accept, especially this kind of mixing up of piety with quasi-superstitious customs ... yet on the other hand it would be wrong to eliminate them all at once – you have to go step by step. Education is a long-term business, and Christ talks of a tiny seed growing only gradually... I often think this particular parable shows Christ's sense of humour: the seed grows during the night as well, while man is asleep, and how surprised he is in the morning, when he wakes up, to find that the seed he has sown has grown all by itself...

On Sunday 3 October, we had the election for the governorship of the state of S. (The governor is the chief administrator of the state.) The *municipes* also voted for their prefects. As in most of the states where elections were going on, the opposition candidates were elected. There was tremendous excitement when people heard the results. Most people said, 'At last the opposition candidate has won... It's the first time we've managed to get our candidate in!' And some, 'If the opposition candidate hadn't got in (in other words, if the election had been rigged) I'd have given up voting for good.'

What one has to realize is that in fact there is a long tradition here of rigging elections. People who have died vote, and the living vote several times – to say nothing of the innumerable convincing stories I've heard of ballot-boxes filled up with 'extra' votes by the supporters of the party in power. But this time we seem to have had the first good result of the 'revolution' of April 1964; the army was in charge everywhere to make sure the votes were counted honestly. And someone wrote up in large letters on the cemetery walls:

'This year we are very sad, because we shan't be voting!'

Everyone is full of hope now, and I only pray they won't be disappointed. The honesty and goodwill of the new men seems assured, as also their concern with the sufferings of those who are poor in so many different ways... But will they be in a position to do everything the people expect, everything that is so urgently needed? There's so much that needs doing: health, housing, drainage, roads, water, electricity, schools, hospitals, highways, unemployment, etc. etc.

The unemployment has reached tragic proportions. Two textile factories (spinning and weaving) had already dismissed their workers 'temporarily' but the boss has now announced that the closure is final. The workers now out of a job feel doubly injured, because the owner used various stratagems to defeat the law: they have really been blackmailed into accepting only a small part of the redundancy pay they have a right to. They should refuse, but how can they? Their families are dying of hunger, and they know that the lawsuit, which has already dragged on for ages, could still go on for another couple of years; and as long as no agreement is reached, the boss will hang on to their work cards, so that they can't sign on anywhere else (if they should be lucky enough to find anywhere).

Yesterday I heard that the 'Fabril', another textile factory, will also be closing in December. What about the trade unions, you ask? Alas, the unions are powerless. There is a recession going on all over Brazil – it's a general crisis which began after the April '64 'revolution'. The government wants to fight inflation, but of course it's the poor who have to pay. One wonders how they can possibly bear any further burden of suffering. *Sa porque Deus é bon*, someone said to me the other day – 'Only because God is good'; and that is their typical response, one of trusting, truly miraculous faith. Or is it, in such circumstances, simply the conformism of

173

fatalism? What is one to do? How respect and promote their authentic faith, while at the same time making them aware that they must fight? Would that the Lord would enlighten us!

Surely a struggle is part of his plan – the struggle to get the poor who are crushed to the ground to stand erect? To make the poor aware of their dignity as children of God, and demand a minimum living-standard to raise them above animals? The other day I had a long talk with Neide at the ACO centre. She is one of the many workers from the Santa Amelia factory which has closed down. She's forty-five and since becoming a lay leader her life has totally changed. She's very much involved in her neighbourhood and very humble, yet a wonderful leader; she's in charge of the Macauba team.

We talk of factory inspectors, unions, lawyers, the workers' response, but what to do, Lord, what to do? What is your plan in all this, Lord? Neide makes a point of never complaining to me, but I discovered shortly after our talk that she had told someone, 'Today, all twelve of us lunched on boiled rice and a miserable few shrimps. For supper we had to make do with coffee.' To which Jose Santos, another ACO leader answered, 'In our house it's *arroz purinho* [plain rice] almost every day.'

Most ACO leaders live in exactly the same sub-human, sub-proletarian conditions as everyone else. The advances they have made, humanly and apostolically, have not alienated them from their fellows. Their presence among the people is a ray of light in the darkness, a sign – perhaps the only one – of hope... The Church of the poor... Are we really one with it?

The other day, two women who are out of work came to see me: 'We can't cope any more; we're worn out from traipsing round the town looking for work.' 'We had nothing to eat this morning,' said one, 'and my kids went off to school without any breakfast.' She was crying, and it was all I could do not to cry too. What is to be done? We could give every penny we have without even beginning to touch the problem – yet sometimes we have to give something. I sent a letter to the new Governor to warn him yet again of the absolute necessity of creating jobs somehow.

Since the elections, the water and electricity have been cut off most of the time. Our evening masses are generally by candlelight. Yesterday I used a glass of water to wash with (our tank is completely empty). And very often there isn't any meat or even fish in the market.

But don't think our morale is low! There's a marvellous atmosphere of mutual help. I'm sure it is terribly important for priests not to be alone. Richard and I have activities which take us off in our different directions – Richard the YCS, myself the ACO; but very often, especially in the evenings, we meet and compare notes, and this is a great help towards seeing things more clearly. Also, most important, as well as our friendly relations with the people (who love their priests), there is our contact with our Catholic lay leaders which sustains and inspires us all.

And what a colourful life goes on around us! We live in a little world full of activity, noisy, motley, and heartwarming in its humanity, its directness, its spontaneity; certainly in one sense, poverty has been defeated already. Even the material side of life seems to be shot through, transfixed, i.e. conquered, by a kind of spiritual intensity... I am sure that Christ will be there in the middle of it – indeed only a fool could fail to see that he's already there. I tell you – the Church of the poor is something fantastic. There are days when one's priesthood seems quite irrelevant and small in comparison.

Take the family: father, mother, nine children. They were buried the day before yesterday by their house collapsing on them during the night. When I got there the place was surrounded by neighbours and friends who had

175

rushed to help. The father said to me, 'God is good. We might have been killed. Everyone's hurt, but no one seriously. We've been spared.' The mother asked me, 'You don't think God was punishing us?' – but the father said at once, 'No, don't say that: Jesus himself suffered and died on the cross, and we must accept suffering too. Today it's us, tomorrow it'll be someone else; everyone has to suffer.'

The association for maids, under the guidance of ACO girls, is continuing with its work of creating awareness, and going from strength to strength. The other day one of the maids asked me, 'Why haven't we got our own ACO group?' Four of five Sundays ago, they asked all their friends to a picnic, and I was invited too.

I still go to the leprosarium at Bomfim occasionally. There's a priest now acting as chaplain, but as he also has a parish in the country he can't get there very regularly. Jorge, the young leper in Santa Teresinha, is much better now. Thanks on behalf of the lepers for all the help promised.

The day before yesterday, our new Prefect came to call at Santa Teresinha. He came to the parish mass and we were glad to welcome him. In the pitch-dark church (electricity cut), he said to Richard and me, 'Well, I'm going to get your hole filled up' (an enormous hole, over thirty feet deep and over sixty wide, caused by the rains last year. . . it's still there, a threat to several houses and to everyone who walks past). . .

On Saturday 27 November it'll be the Governor's turn; he's promised to visit us too.

Well, I've had a lot to say today. I haven't even asked 'How are you all?' yet. Pray for us – we can do nothing without your help; and keep on backing us up with your friendship.

LETTER

To his family: Today I'm back with my beloved lepers, at Bomfim. I've just been with one who's waiting to die; it was horrible; he's yellow like an old wax candle, and his leg is hideously eaten away. You have to make a great effort not to avert your eyes. When will the moment of truth arrive? When will the defeated, the damned, the condemned, the victims of this world rise up in final victory? How much longer will the victory seem to lie with baseless appearances?

9 p.m. All is peace here – apart from the inevitable loudspeaker retailing cheap music; luckily the hellish machine isn't as close to me here as it is at Santa Teresinha. I've decided to spend the night here, because this evening's ACO meeting has been cancelled: I'll only go back to town tomorrow... Today, the *Imaculada Conceiçao*, is a holiday all over Brazil; all the shops are shut and there are masses as on a Sunday. This evening, after mass, I went round giving communion to the lepers. I can't express the joy I felt. You have to be a bit mad to be a priest – and if you aren't, you have to become so. The priest's joy is a mad joy, and only madness makes it possible. I've never managed to destroy my power to love, and indeed I think that, on the contrary, my heart has grown larger rather than smaller; it's larger, and in spite of all my faults, it's growing larger still. It seems to me frightful that a priest, because he is celibate, should ever become an embittered 'old maid' of a man; I can't bear to believe it. In fact, I feel more like a child, who discovers new wonders every day, who starts loving all over again every day, who never stops loving or believing in love, and whom life cannot therefore really hurt.

LETTER

To his family and friends: It's a long time since I last wrote. I'm taking advantage of the peace of Bomfim to call on you again. I've gone into hiding here to prepare a retreat which Fr Lucio and I are going to preach during Holy Week to the ACO members and workers in the city.

Since my last letter a lot has happened. In January there was a meeting in São Paulo of French priests working in Latin America. Eighty came from every part of this vast continent: Brazil, Chile, Argentina, Bolivia, Uruguay, Venezuela.

Here's a paragraph from the letter Pope Paul VI sent us for the occasion:

'We are happy to think of this meeting which will bring together, in a spirit of brotherly understanding and mutual charity, the French priests now working in the South American continent. This meeting will remind you all more forcefully of the bond between each of you and your diocese of origin, with the bishop who has sent you, and with whom you must still feel a relationship of filial unity. At the same time, you will strengthen your sense of union with the diocese where you are now working in close contact with other priests, and sharing with them as far as possible the same conditions of life and work, in the same obedience to the bishop, making the same efforts to put the conciliar decrees into effect.'

It was a most exciting meeting: we were able to reflect on our mission here, with Bishop Riobe and Michel Quoist who made a special trip for the purpose; we were able to exchange ideas, compare difficulties and experiences, and share our hopes. And it was deeply moving each evening when we met round the same table like eighty brothers to offer and eat the same Bread. Weak as we may be, we are inspired by the same strong determination to carry this Christ whom we receive to all our brothers in Latin America. You may have seen our collective letter to our bishops in France. There's one bit in particular I'd like you to note: 'On coming here we were thinking of "giving", of "bringing", but we can now say, "It is they, the poor, who have taught us the gospel. For every one of us the close presence of the poor is a call to the evangelical life, and also the profound source of our joy." '

There's another question: are we, the 'rich', really concerned over the suffering of the poor? Do we tend to forget that our comforts are *directly provided* by the want, the hunger and the suffering of our brothers in the Third World – simply because our international structures are so designed?

During this meeting I had the pleasure of seeing again a priest-friend who is working in Chile, and Michel Duclerq who travels all over South America sowing the seed among teachers, and so many others – to say nothing of the many new friends we have also made.

In February I went with a delegation of five leaders from S. to take part in the first regional ACO meeting. The ACO is very conscious of the need to become decentralized: we have laid the foundations for a regional ACO in the north-east. During this meeting, both leaders and chaplains discussed the appalling conditions the working class endure in the north-east, with case-histories to provide illustrations of this, and above all the lack of security in jobs. We produced a 'manifesto' to be sent to all workers, the management, the public authorities and the Church. I think that if you read this manifesto you will find it easier to get the picture of what the north-east and our work here is like – and it may inspire you to pray even harder! Here are some selected extracts:

4. The meeting has made it clear that the situation of the working class in the north-east is characterized primarily by a *contempt for man*. That contempt, of which the workers

are the victims, is expressed by an atmosphere of all kinds of persecutions – cheating over wages, frequent dismissals, decisions directly and deeply concerning the lives of the workers being made without even consulting them, exploitation of miners, people being given work heavier than their physique can cope with, etc. etc.

11. This atmosphere with its injustice, its contempt, and its lack of respect, has profound repercussions on the worker's life, on his family, on the whole working class, on the community and on the country. The worker finds himself unable to carry out his responsibilities. Workers' organizations are weakened and in danger of collapsing altogether, because of course the first victims will always be the really committed members. The working class is losing faith in authorities and institutions. The unity of the family is affected since it finds itself without means of subsistence.

12. A worker in the face of so much injustice is a man without freedom, without a future, without hope, or faith, or love. Insecurity is destroying him, or turning him into an angry revolutionary. The more humiliation he suffers, the more his productivity goes down, for he becomes emotionally unbalanced and his health and temper become affected. He feels unrespected, worthless, weak and useless.

Worn out, and with no more faith in protests or demonstrations, he can see nothing in life to fight for, and often simply goes to pieces, taking to drink or other vices. He loses faith in God and man. He is obsessed with the fear of losing his job, and is so defeated that he would rather submit to humiliations and loss of dignity than have no work at all and go hungry. In this situation of shame, he is a beaten man for whom work, far from being a means of realizing his dignity, is a bond of slavery, a necessary evil in a life filled with suffering. He no longer believes in the higher things of life – truth, justice, brotherhood, and so on – because in his own life these things are non-existent.

13. The insecurity of this working life has certain inevitable repercussions on his everyday life at home: misunderstandings, arguments, scenes. The children are obliged to work almost from babyhood, and the daughters may well be forced by circumstances to become prostitutes. From time to time a man like this, despairing and shattered, will leave home and seek refuge elsewhere – just to get away from the sight of his hungry children, his ill-tempered wife, and a home where there is no food and no kind of comfort. These are the homes where lying becomes a way of life, and thieving begins from childhood. The family itself is destroyed, because it lacks the necessary conditions in which to discover and fulfil its own ideal.

17. If you look at the consequences, you can see that such a situation is essentially anti-human and anti-communitarian; it lacks the basis on which to build a human life.

19. How can a worker whose sole preoccupation is keeping alive possibly think about developing human and spiritual qualities? As one man put it: 'How can I reflect or think when I look at my hungry children and my empty larder?'

We're surrounded by materialism. People no longer believe in man and when that happens, they can't really believe in God any more. We see constant evidence here of how this situation affects spiritual and religious life – for the perfecting of man and the coming of the kingdom are one and the same thing and can only happen together. Precisely for that reason, it should not surprise us to find that Christ's supreme teaching was that we must love our fellow-man, if our love of God is to be authentic.

On our way back from Recife (four whole days there, and four back, by bus, on rudimentary roads – not so much a journey as a major expedition!) we stopped at T. where, with the support of Dom Joaquim, the archbishop, we have launched the ACO with a group of adults. We have promised to follow up the enterprise (T. is only a day away from S. by bus).

With Yves's return in January our team was complete again, but now Richard has gone on leave to France in his turn. Some of you will certainly have the pleasure of seeing him. While he's away, Yves is taking over the YCS, and I the university group (I was with them for a year before Richard himself took over).

Life goes on, with all its daily worries and struggles. A new ACO group has been started, another is being formed and a third is planned. It is becoming quite a problem to follow up all the teams, some of which are in quite distant sectors. Public transport is most inadequate (ancient buses, few and far between, and some Volkswagen mini-buses; but after eight o'clock in the evening, there's virtually no transport at all in Santa Teresinha), so we have to make up for it by walking. Since there are so many teams being formed, what we are working hardest on is the training of leaders. In my programme (in addition to meetings which take place every evening) I fit in a visit to one or two teams weekly and spend the whole day in the district concerned.

The other day I visited Salina de Lira in this way, a place where almost all the houses are built on the mud. The people there are the poorest of the poor – yet how direct, how warmhearted, how open they are! One woman said to me, 'I haven't gone to mass for a long time, Father, I've been to confession and communion once in my life. When I lived in the country I used to go to mass, but I didn't understand a word the priest said – the only thing I did understand was that everyone bowed their heads when the priest held up the consecrated host; but I didn't – I raised mine so that I could look at it, because that was something I *could* understand. All the rest of the time, I said my prayers. The church is some way away now, and I say my prayers at home, and we say the rosary together. But Father, when we have our ACO meeting each week, don't you think that is a mass?' I was enormously moved by this, because I feel just the same way about it myself. With her absolute simple faith, her poor woman's faith, pure and profound, she had got to the heart of the matter: the encounter with the ACO is an encounter with Christ – it is the way she meets Christ in her everyday life. When the ACO group meets, it is Christ bringing the community together to hear the Word, to hear the calls he makes to us through life; it is Christ really present (where two or three are gathered together in my name ...), Christ using our work study sessions to send each of us out on our mission. Yes, that is a mass all right. I don't think I'll ever forget that conversation I had with her in her rickety little hut in the mud, with pigs and dogs scrapping in the street outside.

The 'Nest' quietly continues its good work among the prostitutes. From time to time ten or so of them arrive at Santa Teresinha, just to say hello to us, or perhaps to have lunch. The maids' association is going from strength to strength with the active help of some ACO girls. There were elections recently and they have a provisional 'committee' (before any constitutions are drawn up, the leaders of the YCW and ACO, who, together with the 'Nest' and the Santa Teresinha youth club, are in the process of setting up boys' and girls' 'artisan centres', are gradually working towards three successive objects: to provide vocational training and efficiency; to encourage and help young people to form working communities within their own occupations; and to help them to form themselves into cooperatives as producers and consumers).

We've had another important event locally here: after endless difficulties and vicissitudes, the various local neighbouring communities and the prefecture have agreed to unite in their efforts to establish a dispensary. Thus the dispensary we set going – thanks to your generosity – which had been taken over by local people who were running it themselves, has now been taken over by the community as a whole (as has all the help we get from France): our enemy number one is paternalism – people *must* do the job themselves!

I shan't go on any longer now – it would be too hard on whoever has to make the copies (especially with the manifesto as well – what a letter)!

Thank you, all who have written – I fear that all too often I have no time to answer – and also all who have sent books and magazines.

My thanks to the ALM for all your generosity and loyal support.

Enjoy your holiday, Richard.

My greetings to you all. We in Brazil and you in France can work to create a bit more justice and brotherly love, a bit more respect for the poor: 'If everyone swept his own bit of pavement, the whole street would be clean.'

S., 10 *May* 1966

LETTER

To his mother: First, a word specially to you. Here in Brazil, Mothers' Day was on 8 May, but Yves tells me that in France it's 15 May. Anyhow, you know with what affection I greet you across time and space: Happy Mother's Day! The day before yesterday, I got to an ACO meeting, and they came and gave me the *abraço* (a hug) and wished me a happy feast! It was so nice – they said: 'This is because your mother is far away, and you can't kiss her today.' I kissed them all for you!

It's raining at the moment, eleven o'clock at night, and I've just got back from a meeting. Along with the rain you can hear the incessant beating of the drums, our normal musical background here. My room has rain pouring in at the window, but by six o'clock tomorrow morning, the sun will be shining fit to bake the stones. It's thundering now. As I went through the Rue São Jose on my way to Jose Maria where the meeting was taking place (Santa Teresinha's third ACO team has come into being), I stopped by to see a sick woman whose confession I heard yesterday. People say she has typhus, but I don't think so. She gazed at me, and murmured repeatedly: 'Padre Paolo, oh, Padre Paolo.' It reminded me of that profound gaze I'd so often had from people who were dying, in la Minotière and la Bastelle – there's a sense of the infinite about it. You feel torn between grief that they must leave everything, and a burning hope – it burns in their feverish eyes which seem fixed on ultimate reality. . .

What's happening about the shop – is it closing down completely? Father must have a lot to see to – I can quite see why he hasn't written lately – not that I am any better – I write even less! But I'm more and more involved with the ACO, which explains, though it does not excuse, my silence. Yesterday we reckoned up: at the present time there are sixteen ACO groups in the city. A seventeenth is to be launched the day after tomorrow at Villa Nova. Then there will be an eighteenth based on the Centre. It all means visiting the members, visiting the leaders, the preparation of meetings, training full-time workers, going to meetings (every day I have to choose among two, three or even four different ones), study days, reports to write, etc. etc. In addition to all this, the ACO of S. are also to help a group recently formed in a neighbouring town – and another in the 'interior'. So, on Friday, I'm off to a place near Rosario in response to repeated appeals from Antonio: he discovered what the lay apostolate can mean through the ACO three years ago when he visited S., and went straight home and founded a group then and there, which is still going strong!

My scooter has certainly revolutionized my life – it's terrific. I waste no more time waiting for buses which are either late or don't come at all. *Le style c'est l'homme*: Yves with his great tough motor-bike; I with my more fragile and elegant Lambretta! The other day there was a funny moment. We were going through the 'zone' (the prostitutes' district), so that I could show Yves a certain garage. We were dashing along, engines roaring, like a couple of James Bonds, till I stopped to talk to a girl who was going to have an operation: in a flash we were surrounded by a dozen of them, all quite delighted to see us. How different from the traditional picture of the dignified and penitential priests of fifty years ago!

It's late, and my hammock looks terribly inviting. My love to everyone, and I'll write again soon.

Yves leaves on Saturday for a YCW chaplains' conference at Petrópolis. I'm hoping to go in June to la Serra for two or three weeks of reading, resting, praying, and listening to the silence!

> Bomfim
> 30 May 1966

LETTER

To his family: It is dreadful to write so seldom, but I know you understand why. The eighteenth ACO group has just been started, and my days are filled with meeting after meeting, rushing from place to place – with all the thousand unexpected interruptions that are the daily lot of every priest to fill in the gaps. I think there are more of these here than in most places, because poverty is a continual call.

Midnight. I wasn't able to finish my letter at Bomfim, because they came to get me, and the boat was actually waiting to take me back to town. I then said mass at Santa Teresinha, and went on to Villa Nova for the ACO meeting. It was raining, so I went on foot instead of by scooter. I went by the *estrada nova* to save time, but found it submerged by the river – the incoming tide had washed away the bridge – so I had to wade through the mud (luckily it was low tide again!) – not easy in a torrential downpour. Yesterday I had a study day with the ACO which was very successful (theme: married life), and in the evening an informal meeting of all the various lay groups was held at the seminary, with the archbishop present. It was a good party.

My trip to the interior went very well. Three hours in the train – one of those prehistoric, 1830 Wild West type trains – another two on horseback, an hour by boat along the beautiful river Itapecuru, and finally another hour on horseback! I had four marvellous days, every minute filled with meetings, official and otherwise, and study sessions. It was fascinating to meet the rural Catholic groups which the people have created among themselves, beginning about three years ago, when one of them came in contact with the ACO in S.; this man was so excited by it that he wanted to start something of the same kind in his village, and it's still going strong after three years without any outside help, and no priest at all.

I must stop here for today – it's very late. All my love to you all, and best wishes to all other relations and friends.

La Serra
12 June 1966

LETTER

To his parents: I'm writing by candle-light. Outside everything is still. I've just been having a long discussion with two German Franciscans about the two world wars, the partition of Germany, the danger of communism, the atom bomb, and our great General whom they do not love. I got here the day before yesterday, and already I feel a new man. At last I'm hearing silence! I can wander as I like among the thousands of little mountain paths; I can pray, read, sleep and even eat regularly. I'm still working my way through Emmanuel Mounier who fascinates me (community personalism) and also the Council documents – which take quite a bit of unwrapping!; I've got some books you've sent me, and a few

187

Brazilian classics. Certainly enough to fill my 'retreat' – it's a real re-charging of the batteries as far as I'm concerned.

I set off from S. for T. last Wednesday, and there I spent a night with the Jesuits. At T. a ridiculous thing happened: I was to continue my journey by coach, leaving at four in the morning. I was suddenly woken in the middle of the night by a group of young men who arrived rather noisily in a nearby room, and on looking at my alarm-clock, saw that it was ten to four. 'The wretches! They never woke me, and I'm going to miss my coach!' I leapt out of bed and dressed, and ran to the coach station. Nothing in sight – obviously it had gone. The brutes! I went up to a jeep-taxi, in the hope of getting it to catch the bus en route; the driver roared with laughter: 'You're leaving at four in the morning? But it's only ten fifteen now!'

Last Saturday at Santa Teresinha we did what has now become a tradition: *romaria* to Riobamba. We left the neighbourhood at about half past eight in the evening and walked all night until four in the morning (about eighteen miles) singing, praying, dancing, talking about the Bible (all those characters who had journeys to make, and often had to leave their homes at night), chatting idly, and looking up at the stars. The people of God on the march! There was a marvellous sense of friendship and brotherhood – as simple as a bit of bread you share with someone which is far better than any fancy cake when you're really hungry. I was the only priest there, because Yves, who hasn't been too well lately, still had to rest.

S., *17 October* 1966

LETTER

To a friend: ... As far as we are concerned, we three priests at Santa Teresinha, we don't live in very grand style... I don't know how we'd manage at all without the help we get from friends and relatives. It's a question of life or death, for all we get from the diocese is Yves's salary, which he gets as parish priest, and that is little enough; our people are too poor to help us much – everything we do for them is free, and they put whatever they can in the box. Do you realize that we have to provide for *all* the expenses of three priests and five nuns – in addition to the many others who come from the country to spend a few days' retreat or relaxation with us here because we're in town?

If the church isn't to collapse completely, it needs a lot doing to it pretty quickly. We also have to give quite a large measure of material support to our lay groups – YCW, YCS, ACO; they could not survive without it, yet it must be given without any hint of paternalism or clericalism. This need directly follows our conviction of 1. the vital importance of local, regional and national meetings etc.; 2. the isolation of S. from the rest of Brazil (it's known as 'the end of the world'); 3. the extreme poverty of the majority of members, especially in the YCW and ACO – without help from their brethren in the developed countries they simply could not take advantage of these important contacts. True, Yves has bought a motorbike and I a Lambretta, but that was only after a great deal of thought; we decided it would be a great help towards increasing our apostolic *yield* without doing anything to invalidate our *witness* (now, six months later, I am pretty certain we were right there). The only luxury we allow ourselves is going out to dinner three or four times a year for a restaurant meal to celebrate a birthday or other occasion.

I'm not telling you all this by way of complaint (we are in fact extremely happy here), but to give you an idea of what our problems are. We discussed it among the three of us, and agreed that, since you had asked, I should go into some detail in writing to you. There are times – often, in fact – when we wonder if we can hang on at all. There are so many other necessary expenses too numerous to mention (for instance the girls from the 'Nest', the prostitutes who 'leave' and then find themselves back on the streets . . .). One prostitute, Jane, spent more than six months with us, and eventually died a saintly death at Santa Teresinha, riddled with cancer. . . Jose, a seminarian, asked if he could spend his last year working with us, as his seminary had closed; we were delighted to accept, but where was the money to feed him to come from?

S., 14 July 1966

LETTER

To his family and friends: The fourteenth of July . . . It is odd to think of the military parades, the wreaths being laid on war memorials, and the brass bands that must be playing their heads off in France at this moment – how the children here would love it all. We don't celebrate 14 July in S., and I'm unmoved at the thought of flag-waving; but my heart still thrills to that great dream of liberty, equality and fraternity. On the one hand, there is narrow nationalism, defence of privilege, pride of place, racial prejudice; on the other, universal brotherhood, a world longing for unity, a great movement stirring all over the world of human solidarity, respect for the poor and mutual help. On the one hand men are shelling and bombing one another (still the flag-waving and how loathsome it is); on the other, human beings are dying because there is no place for them – no food, no work, no housing, no hope. They are truly 'the wretched of the earth'. Get my parents to show you the photos of the new shanty-town now being built at Santa Teresinha, and see if you aren't appalled at the thought of the Bomb – and the bombs. Look at the children with swollen stomachs (they all have worms), the consumptives, the lepers, and the anaemic; listen to the frightful groans of such poverty, let it penetrate right into your hearts, and see if you aren't sickened after that.

Yes, a new *favella*, a new shanty-town (only one more among many) is growing fast, like a monstrous cancer on Santa Teresinha. Hundreds and hundreds of stilt-huts, above the mud created by the incoming tide. At high tide most of them are completely cut off by water, except where people have built a narrow and rickety foot-bridge out of planks... When the planks break you find yourself flailing about in the water or mud below. These are all poor people who have only recently come from the interior, or from another district where their hut was too small, or the rent too high, or they were given notice to quit, or they simply want to build another hut and try to make a bit of money by renting their old one.

Poor things – they really tear at your heartstrings. Whenever I go down there I think of all that will happen to them: of this man who'll be bedridden in two years' time with TB, and that woman who'll succumb even sooner with the everlasting humidity and total lack of hygiene. And right now, this child, weeping: 'No, Padre, it's nothing; he fell into the mud yesterday and he's still got some in his eyes.' Poor kid, what he's got is the beginnings of glaucoma. How soon will he be blind? His pupils will harden, and then... And what is that sudden appalling stench? It's quite unbearable; right next to one wretched hut where people sleep, eat and live, someone has left a dead horse, not buried it, just left it there! Fortunately there are some *urubus*, a type of vulture, constantly circling round the town in search of carrion, and they do their job pretty well. Crabs in the mud; my meditations lead me to see how true is Jose de Castro's comparison with the 'cycle of the crab'. If you look on a map, even a very recent map, you see no trace of the hundreds and hundreds of people who are living here – on the map there is only *mangue* ground covered periodically by the sea, where human beings *cannot live* – only crabs. If I were to go and talk to the Prefect about them, he would look at the map: these people do not exist; there are no people there; there are only crabs. And if I were to go to the bishop, he would say, 'What parish should we put them in? There hasn't been anyone there before; up to now they haven't been anyone's responsibility.' I look at them and think: quite right, *they do not exist*. There are no human beings here; there couldn't be; only crabs. Developed and improved crabs, rather over-sized crabs. In fact there are crabs of two kinds – large and small. The large live on top of the mud, the small underneath it; but it's the same mud they all crawl about in. When the large ones are hungry, they eat the small ones, because they have nothing else to eat. And when they've finished eating, they throw what's left (and their own excrement) out to the small ones, who rush to eat it. Thus fed, the small ones grow fat, and when they are fat enough the crabs who live above them catch them and eat them in their turn. Nothing is wasted. . .

The poor always understand one another. The crabs eat each other, but fundamentally they are all good friends. Living so close together makes them used to one another, and makes it possible for them to appreciate one another. If you have the same origin and the same fate in store, you have a kind of instinctive, biological, really basic fellow-feeling that draws you together.

The big crabs do exactly the same as the little ones; they are born, they grow, they move round in the mud, and they die. The one moment of drama is when they are drawn by that mysterious force which unites two of them so that other crabs can be born who will live that same life in the mud, so that when they are gone there will remain other crabs. They are in a hurry to unite, so as to make sure of keeping something alive in the mud. They hurry, for their flesh needs the mud, and the mud needs their flesh; it's the crab's life-cycle, and *it must go on*. It is hateful; it is hot – my head is spinning; I can still see the putrefying flesh of that horse. I also see the smiling, graceful faces of the small children, and, above all, their eyes which shine with intelligence and look searchingly for joy. But I can also see the skeletal bodies of other little children – their disproportionate legs looking as if they're going to crack apart, with a great knot of knees in the middle. Oh Paul, you mustn't think too much. Thinking is a luxury – and anyway, what is there to think about?

Two girls call me – cautiously I work my way across a muddy stretch : 'You're all right there – it's dry.' I go in and chat with them. They have arranged their 'house' very well. They are very nice. I think of the girl of twenty, looking like someone straight out of Buchenwald, who's waiting to die in the old parish dispensary. She also once lived in a house like this one, on stilts. God, it's unbelievable that all this youth, health and beauty should be thrown away like this in the mud. You have to be careful, because the plank may break – sometimes you break a leg, sometimes not. The poor are lucky. They cross over these planks dozens, indeed hundreds of times, to get water, or to buy paraffin, to visit their friends – they're always crossing them, and they very seldom fall. They're lucky.

A man is working alongside the footbridge. He is digging in four stakes, the beginning of his house. He's up to the thighs in mud, 'riveted to the spot', as you might say. My eyes blur; this man is just so much mud, a kind of stake set into the mud, only it moves a bit. How long will it last? I come back a different way, and find more work going on – but here, how marvellous to find they are happy ! 'Yes, Father, we're all working together. We're not relations, but we're friends, and we all work together to build one man's house, and when that is finished we all build the next one. We could never do it so well on our own.' How wonderful. I stand there, drinking in their words; I stay quite some time, standing silently with my feet apart, long enough to dream of poverty being defeated, long enough to confront poverty with the obstinate silence of hope, long enough to challenge poverty with the ultimate conquest of love... Love can do anything. Love can transform everything – the poorest, most helpless, most humiliated man can, through love, become aware of his value, his dignity, his mission as a man. It is love that draws the community together; with love the poor are rich, and without it the rich are poor. No, I don't miss the comforts of home – if you have possessions you are preoccupied with the fear of losing them; the poor have nothing to lose. The other day I saw three houses burnt to the ground – it didn't take long to get the contents out! Such people have a lot to teach us about death: death is not the terrifying thing to them that it is to us in Europe – not the frightful worst of calamities. Far from it. Here death is a friend you meet at every corner of the street; you stop to chat with him; he's a regular visitor with clients in every house. 'Being born and dying are the usual things here,' someone said to me three or four years ago – and I'll never forget it. 'What is the exception, Father – what is abnormal and temporary, is surviving...' Life – survival – what a battle! But one day their deliverance (death) will come, and friends and neighbours will meet and spend the night singing; they'll play cards, and dance, and organize the customary social entertainments...

One day I asked a man – an ACO leader – what he thought of this attitude to death, whether it didn't strike him as a pagan one; he answered: 'If you really believe in the resurrection, and that the next life is the most important one, then you shouldn't be saddened by death, but made happy.'

That day, on my way out of the Rue Epita cio Cafeteira, I heard someone calling me: 'Padre! don't you recognize me? I've moved. See, I'm building a new house.' He was very proud of it – and indeed I must say that these people do produce the most marvellous results. A very poor house indeed, but well built, and clean. I congratulated him. His eyes shone.

'And look, Father, I've got a *quintal bonito* [a lovely gar-den]!' He showed me through the back window. Alas, all I could see was mud and crabs. 'Yes, I've had to leave the ACO team at Salina do Lira, but it doesn't matter. Do you know what I'm going to do? I'm going to start a new team here.' I smiled my answer – I couldn't speak for emotion; happiness sometimes seems like a knife in your heart. I wanted to cry, or to dance in the mud for joy. I looked at our church in the distance, a hideous erection of bricks and cement up on the hill, and I felt that ugly and poor though it is, it's still too patronizing up there. It's too far away. The church should be down here; it *is* down here. Among the poor. If I'm really a priest, this is where I must be.

... This is the kind of way in which in S. the ACO (which is a totally popular movement, representing the enormous proportion of the people who are of the sub-proletariat) is gradually spreading and expanding with life. At present we have eighteen teams in S. – with a meeting a week each! The full-time workers, Maria and Sebastiao, are wonderfully dedi-cated, and some of the leaders of long standing recognize their responsibility and are coming to the help of the burgeoning groups. Luckily I am now 'motorized' (as also is Yves), and my Lambretta is a wonderful help in getting to meetings and travelling from one district to another.

I recently had the joy of taking part in a second meeting of the regional ACO team (for the north-east region) in Recife. It was great. We took the opportunity to consider how far we had been able to act upon our Manifesto (which I trans-lated for you last time), and what the reactions had been. It has aroused the enthusiasm of our members everywhere, and has made it possible to explain things far better to the public authorities and the employers; it has also helped us to make great strides in arousing the working class. In S. a delegation of lay leaders were to present the Manifesto to the Governor, the Prefect, the Archbishop, the District Commissioner and

195

the Inspector of Works. It has been handed out to all the organizations of workers, unions, cooperatives and neighbourhood communities. Above all, we have really studied it in our groups, and it has resulted in a tremendous upsurge of activity among workers, especially as regards security of employment, and other conditions of work. We are now preparing a second manifesto to be a sequel to the first, more simply written, containing more facts, and proposing more concrete action (in so far as action is possible in face of all the obstacles). We're also preparing a training leaflet for team leaders; I've been given the section on the Church's social teaching to write.

S., 26 October 1966

LETTER

To his former parishioners and friends: My last letter was on 14 July – how lazy I've been. But, as we all know, the longer you keep at it, the more work there is to do. I'm sure you don't hold it against me.

The ACO flourishes (eighteen groups in the city, seventeen of which meet weekly, the eighteenth monthly). We have to plan meetings, visits, discussions, training for leaders, study days, etc. One team has started up in the next state, and that has to be visited (a day's journey by bus, nearly two hundred miles) and followed up.

There is a rural lay Catholic experiment under way in the interior of our own state, alongside the ACO, and that must be followed up too.

Last week, our archbishop asked me to go with him on a pastoral tour organizing youth meetings on the theme: 'The awakening of the laity to the apostolate'. On the way, we got stuck four times, and found the road blocked by sand; we had to dig ourselves out and lay branches down under the wheels, etc. Even the archbishop took off his cassock (and realized that it didn't lessen his dignity by one iota), and helped, with a knotted handkerchief on his head to keep the sun off, which gave him a splendidly comic appearance. I took a snap of him, but you'll only see it if you come to S. !

Since he was deploring the fact that he couldn't buy new tyres because the diocese was so poor, I took the liberty of saying (in the spirit of the catacombs, which he shares): 'But, your Grace, why don't you sell the archbishop's palace then? It's huge and hideous – it's impractical for you and off-putting for us, and it makes you look like part of a triumphalist and established Church. You could live in a far simpler house, closer to the people, and then you'd have enough money to buy three or four tyres a year, and other things too.' An Italian Capuchin was listening and looked thunderstruck, whether because he was a Capuchin, or because he was an Italian, or both, I don't know. The trouble is that we tend to get far too easily used to being established. We're all the same: we give ourselves totally and generously to begin with, and then, bit by bit, with the most legitimate reasons, we gradually take back first this and then that... The Lord knows that I, too, who once gave myself completely, and did so again in coming to Brazil, often try to take back some of my gift in this or that little way. One must never stand still, never get into the *habit* of anything (that's the worst thing of all); every morning we must set off afresh, begin all over again, with a new heart, new eyes, a new enthusiasm for life.

I much enjoyed this contact with the young people in the countryside; they are ready and waiting and looking for something to do. They realize that their own future, the future of the north-east and the future of the Church form a single whole, and that that whole is in their hands. We need leaders, and to get leaders, we must create awareness. Leaders must come from among the most destitute, so that the poor may become aware of their own human value. Leaders to arouse the north-east and get rid of sub-proletarian conditions, large-scale hunger, slow and premature death, unemployment and despair. Leaders to enable the Church of Christ, the Church of the poor, to assume and sanctify all the Indian, African and Latin elements that go together to form this particular mentality. To say that the poor are not cultured is true only in a limited sense: they have not received any culture as individuals, in any sense that would enrich and develop their own individuality ... but in their blood, with their mother's milk, they have acquired a whole gamut of values, a special form of understanding and sensitivity that comes from the civilization of their forbears. For instance, the poor in our district display responses and collective attitudes which are clearly Indian, or clearly African in origin... The Church must be present *within* so as to reveal to them that all that is good comes from Christ and is a preparation for the kingdom ... to rectify or purify whatever is amiss ... and above all to help towards the development of the cultural wealth of a unique people whom the Church needs if her expression is to be complete and perfect.

Yves and I often spend almost all night talking, and we have become quite convinced that evangelization means the continual creation of small communities. Communities of every kind. Whenever St Paul visited a city or an area, he left a community behind when he went, a community that was to go forward and develop. It seems to me that evangelizing means communicating a vision, a new vision, that uncovers the deepest meaning, the 'religious' significance of the world, of things, of events, and of people. Now the normal way towards achieving such a transformation would seem to be through the community. Conversion is a personal step forward, but it is also a collective step forward, because whole outlooks have to be converted. (As Cardijn used to say, you mustn't just catch the fish one by one, but change the water too.) Jesus made some clay, and 'touched' the eyes of the man born blind, who was at once able to see things. But he also spent a long time in the gradual training of twelve ordinary men; bit by bit, with enormous patience, he helped them to think about life, death, work, love, the family, poverty, destiny, and so on.

He began by taking them as they were, with their own scale of values, and slowly helped them to reassess their 'collective outlook' in relation to the scale of values that belongs to the kingdom. . . This is fundamentally what we are doing in the ACO and YCW, discovering the 'natural communities' – the bonds that link people together – in which they think together, live together, respond together, etc., and, having discovered them, making the best capital out of them – for whenever people unite and strive for something beyond their own self-interest, God is there. One can suggest that together they study their life, a wonderfully helpful practice, as John XXIII reminded us : looking at life attentively, really scrutinizing it and seeing what we can discover; listening to the gospel, 'quarrying' at the word of God and meditating upon it with an almost passionate intensity, so as to see how it links up with life, what light it casts upon life's mystery. And all this *in community*.

The Lord is present, and present in two senses :

1. The poor who love one another – God is there.
2. The poor who are seeking God – God is there.

'God spoke of old to our fathers by the prophets; but in these last days he has spoken to us by a Son.' To this I am tempted to add, 'And last of all, he has spoken by the poor.' God reveals himself, he calls to us *in* and *through* the community. I am a priest, and I take in a great many meetings as chaplain when, of course, I have to speak. But it's only when I'm silent that I hear God speaking.

Recently I took part in the national meeting of the ACO. It is expanding fast, especially in the north-east, in the São Paulo area and in the Rio Grande do Sul. In a few days I am leaving for F. with Maria and Pedro (for a regional team meeting).

You will have heard what has been happening lately in Brazil (the workers' and students' activities, and the bishops' statement). The statement of the bishops of the north-east, which caused so much of a stir, was itself inspired by the Manifesto of the north-eastern ACO. A great deal has been achieved in all this – a greater awareness among the people and a renewal in the Church. But it's hard to see what the future holds ... the north-east is really simply a colony of the south, and Brazil as a whole is a colony of international capitalism with all the economic exploitation that entails. For instance, our state is almost as big as France, but its population is rather less than an average *département*, and the poverty everywhere is appalling. Why? Why, Lord, when the place has rich soil, a wealth of minerals, plenty of water, plenty of sun? The *babaçu* alone (a palm tree of which there are acres and acres) could of itself provide for most of the needs of the people, the experts say...

Yet the state of S. only 'earns' from its *babaçus* the few cruzeiros to be got from the primitive labour of breaking the shells to get the nuts out... Oil, pharmaceutical products, paints, drugs, food products, and the thousand other industrial by-products of the *babaçu* – all these are manufactured abroad!

What we need is a radical change in structures and in outlook. The privileged must be willing to reconsider their privileges in order to arrive at a minimum justice for all. But they can only do it if the outside world stops interfering!

The absolutely vital thing is to carry on patiently with the work of training leaders from among the very poor, and make our communities aware of their potentialities. There lies our only hope. There will then be a leaven ready for the Lord to use at the moment of his choosing. Tomorrow? Yet I shouldn't speak of 'tomorrow', for it has begun already today.

Every time there is collective action in a neighbourhood or in a workers' organization, a blow is struck for the future of Brazil and for the Church.

Did you hear that Fr Lucio (with whom I spent several months when I first got here) has been appointed national chaplain for the YCW? – fine for the YCW, but of course one priest less for the parish work of the diocese...

The 'artisan centres' organized by a number of ACO and YCW leaders are slowly but surely being set up in different parts of the city. Our last meeting (of the coordinating team) was at the Bomfim leprosarium, and included the Sisters and the principal leaders. We talked a great deal, not primarily to find out what we were going to do, but first of all to pool our experiences of what we had already done. And that's a great deal !

What these Centros Artesanais are doing, therefore, is not so much creating anything new, as reinforcing what is already being done, providing more effective conditions and a wider scope, and giving a community a new orientation and training (working groups, cooperatives, etc.). Our thanks to all the friends who are helping us with this.

Yves is in the throes of taking up (or rather getting his Sisters to take up) hen-keeping. Up to now, thanks to the kindness of all of you, we have kept ourselves solvent, but we have heavy burdens, and can expect no help from our people here, who live in intense poverty. Perhaps we'll make our fortune selling eggs – who knows?

Yves has been badly had, however. The other day he bought ten young hens. 'They sound like cocks,' he told me. And the neighbours were not slow in asking, 'But Father, why have you bought cockerels?'

The shanty-town I wrote about last time (the neighbourhood being built on stilts in the mud where the tide comes in) gets a lot of visits from us: we have to be there, and help them to think out their lives, to form a community. Every

Sunday afternoon everyone meets, and the people are combining to build a hut, on stilts like the others, but a bit bigger: it's the local hall which will also be used as a church.

The other day I saw a woman who had just had a baby: there were two hammocks in a hut made entirely of palm leaves, a single room, with no proper floor but only three or four planks which you had to walk along very carefully to avoid falling into the water and mud beneath. Her neighbours said, 'But you'll die here.' Her answer was simply, 'No, I must fight to live.'

By putting up their huts in the mud, at least the poor avoid having to pay any rent, and this 'economy' makes it possible for them to live a bit longer. Hunger... Who among us is hungry? What fathers or mothers see their children crying day after day from hunger?

The other day, one man couldn't stand it any longer – it was too much for him. He was in the butcher's shop and asked for a couple of pounds of meat; he left without paying. A week later, he came to buy a little more meat, and this time he said, 'You must add the meat I had last week which I didn't pay for. That day I couldn't bear to watch my starving children any longer, and when I came out, I said to myself: either I'll take the meat, or I'll kill him, or he'll kill me, but I can't go on like this. No one could.'

I know one man who labours painfully, up to his thighs in the mud, to catch crabs which he sells in the city (fastened to each end of a stick which he carries across his shoulders); he, his wife and their children only get food if he manages to sell them. When he is sick, or can't go out for crabs, *no one in that house eats.*

I must stop. I could go on telling you thousands of stories like that one. Luckily there are some wonderful stories too – of solidarity, of mutual help among the poor, of responsiveness to others and hunger and thirst for God.

Yes, the Lord is at work in the hearts of the poor and the humble ... he is always there before us.

Yesterday the Superior General of the Sisters of Providence arrived from France. She has come to see conditions for herself before sending any Sisters. Today she went round Santa Teresinha with me, and could only say: 'I'm simply overwhelmed. No one in France could imagine anything like this.' She had to be careful not to fall into the mud ... the footbridge is so rickety.

Very often the ACO members or my parishioners will ask me about France; I can assure you that they think very highly of you, and I can only beg that you will turn your minds and hearts to your brothers in South America from time to time. They really are wonderful people. I sometimes find myself wondering, 'Who can really prove that the civilizations that are highly developed industrially are superior to the underdeveloped areas? We may think ourselves better ... but what guarantee have we that the rich countries won't be destroyed by the very logic of their unlimited appetites, by devouring one another savagely, as they have already begun to do?'

Père Duval's song puts it well: 'The good people have never had their full share of love ... but there is anger rising up on earth as in heaven, anger rising up, the anger of the Lord! ...'

The other day, at a meeting we were meditating on the text: 'Consider the lilies of the field...' One of the ACO girls said with deep feeling, 'I think myself that if Christ came back today, here to this neighbourhood, he wouldn't say that any more. He couldn't. He'd tell us not to put up with it, not just to sit back, but to fight.'

Well, with that I leave you. My best love to you all.

S., 9 May 1967

LETTER

To his parents and friends: It is hard to know where to begin
– there is so much to say.

I might perhaps start by thanking the ALM for their continual help, through friendship, prayer, and material assistance too. I feel convinced that it was largely your special
prayers in the first few days of May that made our *passeata*
on 1 May such a success. I'll tell you about it.

For some months now, the ACO in S. have been trying to
make more contact with the real natural leaders of the working class: the non-Catholics, the non-Christians, and everyone else who is working to improve the situation of the
workers – but *not* by gathering them into the ACO. Making
contact with people does not mean forming them into cells,
or 'winning them over' (in any sense of recruiting them)
which would be deplorable, but acting together, recognizing
their latent worth, working out agreement over such universal and vital tasks as the defence of human dignity and
humanity itself, and the fight for justice and respect for the
poor. It was with this in mind that some ACO workers had
an idea, about the middle of April, of 'doing something' on
1 May with the whole working class. I may say that nothing
of the kind has ever been done before.

Alas, 1 May is usually just a chance to organize masses,
dances, bean-feasts and football matches. Many of the trade
unions are completely bureaucratized, and think only in
terms of do-gooding – totally excluding any possibility of
making demands or fighting to change the structures. Which
is why the great mass of workers has no confidence in the
unions and makes no use of them. The initiative of these few
ACO people snowballed. A first, preparatory meeting, followed by a few more, attracted an increasing number of
workers, with 110 or 120 attending the final one. These meetings were of the greatest importance in creating collective

awareness. The majority agreed to organize a *passeata*, a kind of mass demonstration out of doors, to march with posters and banners, and concentrate in the centre of the town for speeches and the proclamation of a manifesto. To realize what such a demonstration means for the working class of this state, you must remember several facts: the unions are *not* representative, the working class is not organized, those who have managed to rise from the ranks forget their erstwhile mates, everyone lives in permanent fear of losing his job, and, above all, there is the general atmosphere that has pervaded Brazil since what was called the 'Revolution' of April 1964, with the domination by the army, the almost total absence of liberty, continual fear of harassment by police and army in the name of the anti-communist myth, etc.

Despite all this, several workers' organizations (unions, local shopkeepers, youth clubs, workers' cooperatives and so on) were willing to compromise themselves; but a great many refused, with the result that a number of workers joined in just as individuals. The police (as is their policy all over Brazil) did everything they could to make the demonstration a failure, by visiting people's homes with threats and intimidation, and so on. On the eve of 1 May, the police called on the presidents of all the unions and the presidents of the Uniaos dos Moradores (neighbourhood communities), while the local deputy Minister of Labour even summoned some of the union presidents to lend force to these police threats...
The organizing committee of the *passeata* went to ask for official permission from the state police, and then the federal police... Some of the workers' leaders I know did not sleep for several nights beforehand, and there were others who could not even eat. Fifteen thousand leaflets were distributed (some of them dropped over the city by plane) urging all workers 'to observe 1 May, Labour Day, by publicly demonstrating, without interference from politicians, against the

injustices laid upon the workers, and their overwhelming problems : lack of work, the high cost of living, the difficulty of getting their children into schools, the threat of eviction, hunger, ludicrously low wages, etc.' The leaflet declared too that it was 'also an occasion to demonstrate the power, the unity and the fighting spirit of the people of the province', which is the reason why the workers themselves organized the *passeata*. The thirtieth of April was entirely spent in the creation of posters and banners, under incessant rain. And on 1 May, to the great surprise of many, particularly I imagine the police, about a thousand workers started out from the pre-arranged meeting point. A silent demonstration, thirty or forty posters and banners, an enormous crowd watching with a look in their eyes that indicated strong approval, and, mingling with the marchers, ten policemen in plain clothes. Along the route there were rockets to draw attention to what was happening (as is the custom in Brazil); then at the end the crowd massed in one square, and the atmosphere was electric. But when João, one of the YCW, began to talk of the tragic situation of the young workers, without hope, without future, without any chance of technical training, etc., one of the policemen came up to push him away from the microphone, saying, 'That's enough now ! I order you to stop !' Then the excitement really began. The crowd began to surge forward, shouting, 'Go on, João, go on !' and 'He has no right to stop you !' When he saw the effect he had produced, and realized how misjudged his intervention had been, the policeman let João have the microphone back. You can imagine what followed – joyful and thunderous applause. Following João came a president of one of the neighbourhood communities who was courageous indeed : he told how the police had come to his house two or three times. 'But,' he said, 'I realized that they had to do their duty. No, they were not trying to intimidate me, or threaten me. I welcomed them politely because they were simply doing their duty; now, today, I am doing mine. I am free; we are free; we have no right to be silent in the face of injustice and poverty ...'

Here is the text of some of the posters and leaflets (they were read on the radio, and reproduced in several papers): 'Progress is here, but poverty is still the same' – 'The people need work and homes' – 'A roof is not a luxury – it is a necessity. We need houses' – 'We domestic workers are not machines or slaves – we are *people* – and we have a right to respect and love' – 'We want to work – but *where?*' – 'The people do not want charity; they want justice' – 'How do I feed my family when the rent I must pay is higher than the wages I can earn?' – 'We want technical training schools' – 'We need: evening classes – transport – doctors' – 'When the poor go to hospital they don't get sheets, let alone medicines' – 'The Americans are sterilizing women – That is a crime and no solution to the problem of hunger and poverty – It is only the privileged few who have a right to life' – 'The poor can no longer keep up with the cost of living' – 'We want *genuine* trade unions' – 'How much longer will peasants put up with not getting their rights?' – 'We have arms and heads; we want work' – 'Uniform costs money – books cost money – there aren't enough school places: a poor man's son cannot go to school' – 'The people are fed up with promises – we have no electricity, no water, no roads, just holes' – 'Domestic workers need proper conditions of employment' – 'Our neighbourhood needs health, transport, hygiene: we demand human living conditions – Freedom, Freedom!' – 'Our neighbourhood must not be destroyed; the poor need houses too!' And many more.

At the end of the *passeata*, a 'manifesto' was declared and handed out. I think it would interest you, so here is a translation:

Appeal to the authorities, the technicians, the bosses, and ourselves, the workers!
Only those who suffer themselves can talk about suffering; that

is why we workers of this state have the right to talk. This *passeata* on 1 May is an attempt to express the workers' protest
AGAINST
Lack of jobs, which gets worse every day; the largest of the few industries which used to exist have closed down, and the new factories opened recently are not enough to absorb anything like all the workers available, nor are there even any trade schools for the young.

The housing problem, which gets worse as rents go up and up, and people are forced to put up flimsy huts in the mud – and they can be evicted even from those. Furthermore, the building of new avenues leads to other parts of the town being swamped with mud from the sea.

Unjust wages which remain far below the cost of living; they are not enough to provide for even one meal a day, especially given the expense of educating children, and caring for the sick.

In many cases, *the ignoring of conditions of employment* in relation to the minimum wage, overtime pay, holidays, compensation, etc., and the fact that there *are* no conditions of employment for domestic workers.

The position of farm workers who are still totally dominated by the *latifundiários* (big landowners) and their agents, without even minimum technical training, education or medical help, nor any security in their jobs, nor any means of defence.

In consideration of the fact that progress and development only favour those who already wield economic power, and that the poor, far from benefiting from such progress, remain untouched by it and are actually getting poorer;

Declaring that there can be no development or advancement unless *human beings* are put first, and that the worker is not an instrument, a machine or a thing, but a human person, with all the rights and duties involved;

Appealing : to the *authorities* to hear the voice of the working class, to foster the good of *everyone*, especially the most underprivileged, to re-frame the laws in line with the people's aspiration to reform our unjust and inhuman structures, and to produce a courageous policy of employment;

To the *technologists* to place their skills at the service of MAN, and to force the institutions to respect the needs of *social* development;

To the *employers*, to become aware of the human value of their workers, and the contribution they make to business as a whole, by carrying out the laws intended to benefit workers;

To *ourselves, the workers*, to have confidence in ourselves, our abilities, our value, the power of our unity;

Let us unite in our class organizations (unions, neighbourhood communities, etc.) to give them real power in the struggle to defend and foster our rights.

I have said a lot about 1 May, because the whole event seems to me to have been of enormous importance. The working class of S. has just taken a big step forward. Up to the very last minute we were wondering what effect the *passeata* would have. During the silent march with all the banners and things, Yves came to me and said, 'This is terrific – there are people from the whole area – something is stirring among the workers. It's a great thing for the YCW and the ACO!'

The ACO is in the middle of another shake-up: the publication of the Statement of the north-east group, which is taking place simultaneously in the nine north-eastern states; it is really an extension of the Manifesto the ACO produced in March 1966, a piece of work embodying all the most essential facts of working-class life.

It is entitled: 'North-East: Development but Not Justice?' and is a warning as well as a condemnation of the massive injustice suffered by the people of the north-east. Progress is slowly coming, true; but the poor, the people who were poor to start with, are still getting poorer, more and more rejected, left out in the cold...

The ACO is organizing a big meeting to launch the Statement which involves major and continuous groundwork, getting it known in the unions, the neighbourhood communities, the various districts, and so on; and also starting discussions, meetings and positive action arising out of the document.

I cannot resist quoting this comment made by one of our workers over the injustice he met in his factory: 'Given the choice, I'd rather die like a man than a coward'; nor this, from a Brazilian writer who gives eloquent expression to the situation of all the poor, all the *marginalizados* of the north-east really, and certainly to the people living in the mud in La Salina: 'Suffering starts to dehumanize us from the moment we stop being aware of it. It has crossed the sensitivity-barrier, as planes cross the sound-barrier. And as the sound-barrier is really silence, so the sensitivity-barrier is indifference. In other words, de-humanization' (Alceu Amoroso Lima, *Visão do Nordesta*).

In the two months since Yves and I moved into the Salina mud where we are now living with a YCW worker in a little straw hut, a lot of people have told us that we are mad, that we shall never manage to change these people, that they are used to living like this and don't mind it, whereas we suffer far more than they do, and so on, and so on. You could write the speech yourselves; the same kind of thing is said all over the world. And they are quite right – we are mad; we certainly cannot 'change' everything at once: the fatalist mentality, the hideous situation these people are living in. Yet our prime object is not perhaps to 'change' anything, but simply to *be* there, to be there in the name of Jesus Christ as a leaven, so that not we, but they, will be changed as a result of the leaven among them which we hope they will gradually become aware of.

Our being here is a kind of madness, the kind of thing one does in a totally desperate situation when one cannot think what to do; when a mother sees her child dying (Yves once talked to me about this and it taught me a lot); she has done all that can be done, consulted every doctor, bought every medicine, and still her child is going to die. She does not know what to do. So what does she do? There is something she can still do: *she stays close beside him*, as close as possible, never leaving his side, watching for the slightest sign from him, and after all, who knows? Miracles can happen.

The incarnation was a kind of madness. When Jesus had said and done everything, he was silent, and just let the leaven act. It seems to me that our presence, which should be a presence of love, should also be a 'revolutionary' presence; in other words, in a country where a priest is still seen as a person of authority, of considerable prestige, the very fact of going to live in the mud, with those society has *rejected*, the very fact that he can be *seen* as expressing his solidarity with them, this in itself seems to increase the scandal and make it more obvious, more 'shocking'. And this in fact may be the solution: gradually, by living among them, to make the poor aware in their own minds, and gradually to increase the understanding of this scandal throughout the rest of society, until there in an 'explosion'. Is not this, possibly, the way to prepare the 'revolution of love'? Certainly, the Pope's last encyclical (*Populorum Pregressio*) strikes a tremendous chord. When it came out, I bought up every copy I could lay hands on and thrust it on everyone I met; and I re-read again and again sections 30 and 31, on 'the temptation to violence', and 'revolution'.

Yves has just left for a congress of YCW chaplains in Belo Horizonte; he'll be in the south for a bit after that for a rest. I myself was to go in May to a meeting of the area ACO team in Recife, but it has been put off till the end of August, just before the National Congress in early September.

In conclusion, I want to thank you all again. Every week brings some proof of your kindness and sympathy. It is only thanks to you that we are able to carry on at all. Even at the level of material survival, we sometimes wonder how we manage it! We 'earn' almost nothing here; almost everything comes from France. And upon the three of us depend the five nuns who work in the parish, a small parish dispensary where we *permanently* have a few old, outcast or ill people, everything to do with social work (doing our utmost to avoid paternalism of any kind), everything to do with Catholic action : YCW, male and female, student groups, the ACO, domestic workers, helping prostitutes. In fact, there is just so much that I could never list it all : catechists, scouts, youth club, labour cooperative, the leprosarium, the prison, the old people's home – it's endless.

I am only pointing this out because one of you asked me to, to give some indication of our needs. The main thing is for you to be *with* us, to understand the point of our being here, and support us with your sympathy.

I must leave you. *Au revoir*, and please write !

S., 20 October 1967

LETTER

To his former parishioners and friends: ... The wind is roaring through the town. One cannot help thinking of sailors in danger, and of the mystery of life and death : struggle for life, struggle for survival. Yet it is *men* who kill; it is *men* who sow the seeds of death. We are haunted and tormented by two visions : the youth of Brazil, condemned to die before their time, and the youth of Vietnam, being bombed out of existence.

Brazil has between 85 and 90 million inhabitants. More than half the population is under eighteen. The average life expectancy in the north-east is twenty-seven; and in our own state it is undoubtedly even lower. (I don't know precisely, but think it is something like sixty-five in France...) In Vietnam thousands of innocent people are being maimed, buried, shot to bits *every day*. Yesterday, today, tomorrow. But why ? why ?

The two visions are really one. In the streets of S. you don't see happy groups of school-children and students calling to one another, carefree, excited, like young people the world over. It is an old city, yet it is full of young people. I love to look at them, I love them, but I cannot forget that they have twenty-seven years to live, twenty-seven years to wait. They have not long to wait. And since there are a few old people, this average is only reached because some will die at twenty, at fifteen or at ten. Indeed when you are told here that some-one is thirty, you think of him as old. And I know a lot of people who at thirty do look fifty or more. At forty you are a real old man, you have outrun the 'normal' lifespan!

Brazil and Vietnam: these are not the 'norms' of nature, the 'limits' of nature; this is man killing man. Under-development, poverty, under-nourishment, war – all these things have the same basic root: economic imperialism (the modern form of colonialism), neo-capitalism, international economic structures that divide the world in two – exploiting and exploited nations. Those on top live better and longer. Those underneath live in suffering and die young.

Have we any right to be resigned to this? We must have a revolution!

Since my last letter a lot has happened, both to you and to us. I'll mention a few outstanding events:

In July we had a study week with all the priests of the diocese on 'the Church and development in the state'. It was very good.

I then went off to P. and T. with two ACO workers. We spent a week in each town. We set up a good ACO in P., based on two natural community groups; in T. the three teams already working were consolidated. We have other new groups planned.

Then a week in F., to give a bit of help to the ACO who have no chaplain at present. I met a number of priests there. The working-class situation is very different from here.

At the end of August we had a meeting of the area ACO

team in C., and that was followed almost at once by the first meeting of the Regional Council for the north-east, also in C.

On 3 September, near São Paulo, the (annual) meeting of the national ACO team opened, which I attended, with several other members from the north-east.

On my way home, I made various useful contacts.

The high point was the great joy of meeting Bishop Huyghe, during an unforgettable day I spent with Dom Jorge, the Bishop of Santo Andre (near São Paulo). It was wonderful to concelebrate with him, to feel that through him I was joining with the whole Church of his area, and thus linking his state with ours. It was marvellous to feel a communion with the universal Church, when we listened together to a talk by a brilliant young economist on the bitter realities of Brazil; and also when we all went together to meet a group of militant workers (they too were bitter); and when in the evening, we had a conference of both clergy and laity.

I then had a fortnight's 'breathing space' in C. before getting back to S., from where, still covered in dust, I had at once to start off again on a pastoral visitation with our auxiliary bishop to R., a little town about an hour from S. by car.

Now – I've told you enough to give you a general idea of what I have been doing lately. During the course of it all there have been some marvellously rich contacts: I almost forgot to mention one important visit – to Petrópolis, where I spent a day with Pierre and Georges, two French priests who are going through their training course there, and will be coming to S. to help us in early 68. So you can see the future is taking shape. If the committee approves, our archbishop may send Yves and me 'into the interior' after our leave in 68 (when the contract that was renewed in 65 ends), while Richard will stay in S., and work with Pierre and Georges.

Here, in S., our work goes on... Yves is deeply involved in

the YCW of which he is now diocesan chaplain. He gets on very well with young people – but also spends a lot of time with the teaching teams, and the work of local community development.

Richard is working toards some new kind of student movement, as the YCS has virtually ceased to exist, and this new orientation has changed his whole working method.

I myself become more and more convinced of the importance of creating real awareness among adult militants in the poor districts. To talk about a 'working class' is likely to bring certain European images to mind. What we have here is a mass of *sub-proletarians*, among whom a privileged few have regular jobs and wages. But even these are 'on the fringe', and take no part, or very little, in the life of the nation.

One thing that delighted me, when I got back from the national meeting, was to discover that in my absence two new base teams were in process of being launched... The movement now has its own momentum...

Yves has also asked me to help several groups of 'teaching teams' in M. This is very important. Teachers too must become aware. Over half of all Brazilians are under eighteen ! ! The whole future of Brazil is at stake here.

Now I want to tell you what has just happened at the *Radio Educadora* (a radio station started by the diocese last year). It is a story that explains a lot of things. You can get a glimpse of just *what* is stirring in Brazil at present, and *how* it is stirring...

I will give you first the facts, then the documentation :

The facts

On the eve of Independence Day, 7 September, Radio Educadora put out a programme which *immediately* produced federal police action : they were forbidden to function (suspended) for eight days 'because they had commented on Brazilian independence' (in other words doubted it).

Radio Educadora's lawyer brought a suit for 'illegal action'.

The federal judge declared himself 'not competent' to deal with the matter (and the irreverent said, 'He never said a truer word').

The archbishop made energetic protests on TV and in the newspapers, and declared his complete solidarity with the radio station and its purpose.

A few days later, the highest authorities in Brasília sent the federal police a telegram, ordering them to let Radio Educadora go back on the air.

Three documents
1). the programme which caused the fuss;
2). the text of the archbishop's protest;
3). the text of a protest leaflet put out by the students.

1. The programme broadcast on 6 September:
Good evening.

Today is the eve of 7 September, the day Brazilians celebrate the anniversary of our independence. The programme, 'Between day and night', wants all of you to consider with us the answer to this question:

'Does this independence we are celebrating really exist? Is Brazil in fact independent? Or, on the other hand, is the independence we are celebrating simply a mirage?'

Let us consider together:

Can one talk of independence in a country where more than thirty million people are starving? Have we any right to do so? Furthermore, we know that of eight million children of school age, only four million actually go to school. And of that four million only four hundred and sixty thousand even finish primary school ...

We ... we, like all the Brazilians in the underdeveloped areas and the 'marginal' states, we who live in the condition of *nonmen and sub-men*; it is up to us to transform Brazil into an independent country!

There is still much to be done in Brazil, friends, for 'a poor village in India is similar to one in Africa' – but a Brazilian village is worse than either of them.

We know in fact that in the Bas-Tocantinos, the landlords and those who rent the chestnut plantations, also hire out the peasants to pick the chestnuts. The whole area is one where bronchial pneumonia is endemic. The children in the valley wear no clothes at all up to the age of fifteen. That is the kind of life people live in Brazil.

... *And we still have the nerve to call Brazil an independent country!*

2. The archbishop's protest:

I was away from the archdiocese on 6 September. Having got back on the evening of the 23rd (from the meeting of the north-eastern bishops) I immediately left for the interior on a pastoral tour. I got back to the town on the afternoon of 2 October.

Only then did I discover, from the auxiliary bishop, that Radio Educadora, our archdiocese's instrument for Christian information, had been suspended for eight days because it was thought to be 'subversive' by the head of the state sub-delegation of the federal police.

Among the steps I took directly was to lay my case in correct and due form before the federal justiciary, who I was sure would examine it with complete impartiality.

What I have to say to this action is in the nature of a PRO-TEST, which I make firmly and confidently, against the accusation of subversion which has been levelled at Radio Educadora.

I protest, *as a citizen*, making use of the right to freedom of thought and expression, guaranteed sacred by the Constitution of the Republic. Every citizen has the right to protest. Above all, I protest, as *Archbishop* of this fine archdiocese of S. in full awareness of my responsibilities as a minister of the gospel of Christ, who is the Way, the Truth and the Life. My friends ... the development of a people or a country is not measured by its industrial production, but by the level of life that ultimately results from that ...

Development, therefore, means: a greater chance to survive birth, less risk of dying in middle age, and greater protection against death in old age. In brief: more security of life at every stage.

What do the massive sicknesses of Brazil represent? If societies in every age, all over the world, have always shown a marked preference for life rather than death, what is the phenomenon, what the unknown force, that makes the Brazilians, as Antonio Caldo writes, 'the friends of death'?

Those unknown forces, my friends, are the forces of destitution, of poverty, of underdevelopment.

Here is a picture of our national poverty:

Between 1939 and 1960 the price of beans rose 5,000 per cent, the price of meat 3,100 per cent, the price of milk 2,733 per cent, the price of eggs 2,200 per cent, the price of rice 2,000 per cent, the price of bread 1,566 per cent. Faced with such increases, there is no area in which wages have increased proportionately. That is the explanation for the hunger and destitution in Brazil: for the misery of our people.

Hunger, underfeeding and malnutrition lower resistance to disease, and also lower the abilities and the productivity of industrial and agricultural workers; they increase maternal mortality and infant mortality, and lead to a massive lack of prosperity.

Let us be under no illusion. Brazil has yet to become independent. The independence which was achieved on that 7 September now lost in the mists of time, was only independence from Portugal. In the interim, other nations have appeared to replace the Portuguese as exploiters ... We are still being exploited and sucked dry by other countries ... BRAZIL IS A RICH COUNTRY! But what happens to our riches? Where is the profit from our coffee, our metals? our oil? our wood? our sugar? our rice? ...

Why are the Brazilian people still dying of hunger and untreated illnesses? What happens to the work of our agricultural and industrial labourers? Why, though they work so hard, do they die of malnutrition?

The truth, my friends, is simple, but it is also hard: Brazil is *still* being exploited by other countries, and by some Brazilians who are traitors and enemies of their own land ...

It is up to us, Brazilians – and we really are Brazilians, because we were born here and love our country – to *make* Brazil independent ... There is certainly no one else who will do it for us ...

The Church of God in this state shows the way to the house of our Father who created the world 'for man, body and soul, and for all men to flourish in and enjoy'; it is a way of justice, of freedom, of peace.

That Church proclaims the truth. Often the truth hurts. What is deplorable is that truth gets mixed up with the bad seed, and it is not always possible to distinguish between the bad seed and the good. Hence the terrible risk that the truth will be uprooted at the slightest excuse.

Christ's message is a message of Life. 'That they may have Life, and have it more abundantly.' In a land of dead men, we must work that they may live.

Since 12 June 1966, Radio Educadora, supported by tremendous sacrifices, has struggled to assist the development of our beloved state, in collaboration with the intentions of the public authorities, private organizations, and above all with *the people who are actually suffering.*

It may have made mistakes. ('Let him who is without sin cast the first stone.') The purpose for which the radio station has been run, that of helping to create awareness and a sense of direction in its audience, is a purely and healthily democratic one. It respects its audience, and wishes to be respected by them. Why should it then be described as 'subversive'? I leave it to our thousands of listeners and friends to reply. I hope that a free and democratic state will reply with courage. I feel certain that I have the support of all my fellow-citizens in the state in this protest. That is all I need.

3. The students' leaflet:

The students appeal to the people

Why has Radio Educadora been suspended?

Because they had the courage to say what thousands and thousands of Brazilians are thinking?

Because that thinking shows the shameful and humiliating reality we are living in?

Because they make it obvious that we have not yet won our independence?

Because they have clearly shown what we must do to win that independence?

YES. For all these reasons – and also: because there are police organizations paid by the people, but working *against* the people.

Because they have spoken aloud the truth which the dictatorship wants to keep hidden.

Because in dictatorships, radio, the press and television are censored, so that the people cannot be told the truth about their situation.

Because in dictatorships it is a crime to tell the truth.

Because they know that an informed people will overthrow any dictatorship.

And finally because there is a dictatorship: the action of the repressive forces in closing down Radio Educadora is a perfect example of the kind of dictatorial régime we are living in, a régime in which people have not even got freedom of thought. But this does not frighten us; on the contrary, it makes us feel like our oppressors.

Therefore, fellow-citizens of this state: *Join with us and fight!*

During the same period a somewhat similar event was taking place in C. (also in the north-east) – or rather an event which links up with this one. The bishop there, following the meeting of north-eastern bishops, gave an interview to a local paper. He spoke of the need for Latin American countries to become liberated from the metropolitan power, i.e. the USA. 'I see', he said, 'in Latin America a vast, oppressed people. There is no need to analyse all the forms of oppression: they are evident to anyone who looks. That is why the first step it must take is that of liberation. And, consequently, the whole population must be made aware of what is happening, so that there can be a complete break with imperialism – economic, political and cultural. Farm-workers, factory-workers, students, all the oppressed must be called upon to achieve their own liberation.

'The courage of the little island of Cuba can be our symbol and our hope. To the extent that the Latin American people become liberated from the injustice, the domination, the imperialism that alienate them at present, the threat of communism will *ipso facto* be destroyed.'

Explaining further his comments about Cuba, the bishop added:

'Like the small island of Cuba, the whole of Latin America depends on international markets, where our raw materials are the object of an imperialist economic game. All the aid from rich countries to our people will never counterbalance the money stolen from us by the continual depreciation of our raw materials, and the flight of capital. . .'

This interview caused both the local and national press to react strongly. There were angry criticisms, but also an important new awareness. Then, too, bishops who give their opinions with courage, who speak up for the poor, who uncover the roots of the problem – these are the prophets the world needs, the spokesmen for those who have no voice, the oppressed. As one collective letter of support for the bishop said in conclusion: 'to be praised by the praiseworthy is good. But to be criticized by the wicked is no shame to anyone!'

Dear friends, I conclude by sending you all my love, and begging your prayers for South America, and for all the Third World. May the Lord show us how to contribute our stone of love to the building up of the new world, today, here where we are.

Alcantara, 28 January 1968

LETTER

To *his former parishioners and friends:* Rather late in the day, let me wish all of you a Happy New Year!

I am writing from Alcantara, the second oldest town in

Brazil, full of ruins and old colonial-type churches. You get here by sea (three hours from S. by sailing-boat, if there's any wind!) and are at once struck by a mysterious sense of the presence of a magnificent but vanished past, an immense burst of life of which traces can still be seen, but as if petrified : life has gone and only the stones remain. This afternoon I went to see the remains, now overgrown by forest, of a huge *fazenda* which functioned during slave days – a fantastic experience. Little paved alleys, old colonial-type *sobrados*, elegant façades, trees growing out of walls built centuries ago, an impressive small fortress commanding the island, with its cannon now buried in grass – the whole thing vividly recalling the earliest days of the state, the great days of the French expedition of La Ravardière in 1612, good times when the French won the friendship of chiefs and of all the Tupinamba Indians, bad times when the Jesuits got themselves expelled from this state (and all of Brazil) for daring to defend the rights of the Indians and to condemn slavery, for attacking the rising economic power of Portuguese business interests – yes, even then !

Why am I here ? And why have I just spent a fortnight in C. in the interior ? And why am I still going to visit various spots within the state to study rural conditions ? Because, as no doubt you know, at the request of our archbishop, and with the agreement of the French Committee, Yves and I are going to work in 'the interior', and I am taking advantage of this breathing space to start discovering the world which I shall be part of in a few months' time. I say a few months, because it will be after my trip to France in April or thereabouts. As you know, Yves and I go back to France every three years, to see you all and get out of our rut. This time Yves is to do a year's course at the missionary school in Lille, and I a few months of courses and conferences, particularly some progress study with the ACR (Rural Catholic Action) chaplains.

It is almost a month since we left the parish of Santa Teresinha. You can guess something of how we feel – we have left a bit of ourselves behind; a bit of our lives – it is only to be expected, for one always ends up loving those one is with, even though a bit of selfishness is mixed with it. Especially the people of La Salina. I learned so much living there; I will never forget them, nor their mud into which I so often fell.

What has happened is that on 20 December last, our successors, Pierre and Georges, arrived in S. after their course at Petrópolis. Pierre will succeed Yves as parish priest of Santa Teresinha, chaplain of the teaching teams, and Georges will replace me as diocesan chaplain of the ACO. I spent some time with him, to help him make his first contacts, get to know the leading workers and the permanent staff, and find out how the movement works. Yves did the same with Pierre. On 15 January, Yves left for Rio to meet his brother Philippe who is also a priest, but ten years older; he is going to work here too (after his course at Petrópolis). That same day I left for C., a little town about two hundred miles away, to take part in the first area ACR meeting for the north-east. I was there till the day before yesterday, and then came on here. To get to C. from S., there is a bus every other day, and 'the train' every other day too. I came by train, and what a poem that is! There can't be another train like it in the world. There is no timetable. It can be four, five, six or more hours late. Sometimes it leaves the rails. Sometimes the axles must be dismantled because of over-heating. Going through the outskirts of S. there are special wooden shutters at the windows, and the passengers must pull them down, because the kids throw stones at them. I am not saying that this is just a precautionary measure because they 'might' throw stones. They *always* do. Every time I have travelled by train in Brazil I have found this to be the case : there is always a hail of stones; nobody minds, because there are the wooden shutters !

At every stop there is an invasion by all the locals, who turn pedlar for the occasion. They sell everything – platefuls of rice with a scrap of meat in the middle (around lunchtime, this one), mangoes, bananas, and any fruit you care to think of, coffee, monkeys, snakes, parrots, to name a few items. But the thing you notice most about the train is the dust. One looks like nothing on earth by the end of the trip.

However, to get back to our north-east area meeting. It was a great success – 110 *lavradores* (farm workers) gathered for three and a half days representing the various north-eastern states, with a certain number of urban workers and students involved in the same struggle for the advancement of the rural working class. Also taking part were eleven priests and four nuns who are already working with them, trying to help increase the awareness of their brothers in the country in the light of the gospel and of the Council documents. I hardly know how to describe the meeting – it was an absolute revelation to me.

The first day there were various reports which gave us a better understanding of peasant life : of the suffering, the injustice that is hard to label precisely, the conditions which are, in effect, slavery. Considering what causes this 'inhuman and dehumanizing' situation (the phrase used by the bishops of the north-east in January 68), it was shown that it results from an archaic and feudal agricultural system, maintained by a group of *latifundiários* who must at all costs preserve their domination, and who can only keep their privileges at the cost of the suffering and death of the peasants.

I should like to quote to you masses of details I remember from that day – the fantastic rents which the big landowners force the peasants to pay for the privilege of cultivating a tiny patch of their ground; the outrageous proportion (often half !) they take from them of their harvest; how the *fazendeiro's* cattle eat the crops grown by the *lavradoros* because the *fazendeiros* don't bother to fence them in, and the *lavrador* cannot speak out; the women who go to *quebrar coco* (break open the *babaçu* husks to get out the coconuts) and how they are exploited and maltreated; whole families evicted and their homes burnt down by the *fazendeiro*, sometimes tortured and even killed (like the seven trade-union peasants who were barbarously massacred a few years ago, *with the complicity* of the police commissioner, to please the *fazendeiros* of the district). For there you have the tragedy: how can the rural worker defend himself and win respect, when *all* those with any power in the area are themselves landed proprietors? The mayor, the police commissioner, the deputy and the judge are *latifundiários as well*.

To try and give you a more vivid picture of the appalling life of a peasant in north-east Brazil, I will translate the statement made by Manuel on that first day of the meeting. Manuel is at present a semi-permanent staff worker on the ACR, and virtually the founder of the ACR in our state (the ACR being the legitimate offspring of the ACO – but that is another story too long to go into here). To give a better picture of a typical labourer's life in the north-east, Manuel collected a series of true stories, and put them together to make up a 'biography': the story of Francisco das Chagas, a peasant in the north-east.

Francisco is his name – he is a very poor man. He came from Ceara with a very large family – twelve children and a thirteenth on the way. Francisco is a very courageous man; having failed to find any land for his *roça* (field), he went to see the local politicians. For he had been told that the Deputy and the Prefect (a prefect being slightly higher than a mayor) did a lot to help the poor. But it was not near an election! The Prefect said to him: 'My house isn't the place to talk to peasants' (*caboclos*). Poor Francisco therefore set off for the Prefecture where he hoped to find some means of influencing the Prefect, for in the area it was the Prefect who 'made the sun shine and the rain fall'.

The Prefect promised that he would try to do something, and told him to come back the next day. Francisco went to the Prefecture every day for a month. But he got nothing. Finally the Prefect began avoiding him. Francisco was in torment because his family were so hungry, and did not even have a roof over their heads. He tried the Deputy, to see whether he might feel sorry and do something. He met the Deputy in a very smart car, just on the point of leaving for the capital, to relax on the beach and enjoy the Carnival. He promised great things, and declared that he would take up the matter himself. Francisco wearily came and went and got nothing. His situation remained the same.

Francisco spent a night wondering what to do. He said to himself, 'Am I a man, or an animal? I must find somewhere to live.' So he went to see the authorities: the judge, the Deputy, the commissioner of police, and said to them:

'Brazil belongs to all Brazilians. This is a large state. I am a healthy man, and I want work; I must earn a living for a large family, and I can't even find a scrap of land to cultivate.'

The commissioner said, 'I'll introduce you to the landowners of the district. They are all my friends.'

As he went along, Francisco thought, 'There is so much unused land that belongs to a tiny number of proprietors who do not cultivate it; that is why so many peasants are so poor and have nothing.'

They got to the landowner's house, and the commissioner introduced him: 'This peasant (caboclo – a term of scorn) is looking for some ground to farm.' The landowner said to him, 'Well, I can offer you some land, but on this condition: I am in charge of everything around here; I am the political head of the district, the commissioner is my friend and so are all the local authorities. Everyone who lives on my land votes for the Deputy I want. Consequently I will only allow you on my land if you agree to be entirely dependent upon me.'

'Yes, sir,' replied Francisco. 'My family and I are all on the point of dying of hunger, so we have no option but to accept whatever you want.'

The owner continued, 'Very well; you will pay a rent of 10,000 cruzeiros a hectare, or half of your harvest, or you will give me several days' work a week. This applies whether the fields give a good yield or not, whether you are ill or well; you and your family must accept my conditions, and obey my orders.' Francisco was obliged to accept, even though he knew it was completely unjust. In his mind, he said, 'Perhaps things will get better as they go on.' He set to work to clear the forest, and then burnt it, to clean the ground. To start with it was just a bit of bare land in the middle of the forest, but seeing how well his work was going, he wanted to increase his production. However, he had debts to pay for clothes, food and medicine he had got from the shop. So he decided to go and see his boss, the owner of the land, and ask if he could borrow some money to improve his land. The boss said,

'You're one of my men, so you can go to the bank with this letter of introduction, and give it to the manager, and explain that you are one of my people.'

The bank manager was very polite, but he told Francisco that he had lent money to *caboclos* before, and they had only spent it on radio sets, revolvers, bicycles, or drink, and then complained that they hadn't got any more. This had made the bank very prejudiced against them. Therefore they could do nothing for Francisco. He told the manager that he had come simply because other farmers had told him that, though it might be very difficult and take weeks, they had managed to get something. However, despite all this, he had no success, and as he went home, he thought, 'Perhaps the manager was right; after all peasants aren't very well educated, and they do do stupid things, and then of course the good ones have to suffer for the bad.'

So he went to see the man at the factory (a rice processing factory). This man used the factory's money to buy rice before it was planted. Francisco offered him his future harvest, thinking, 'I'll get the money at once, and with it I can clear my ground, buy seed, and still have something over to feed the kids.'

He was a courageous and enterprising farmer, and cleared twenty hectares, but he could not cultivate more than ten, and even those he found almost more than he could manage. The purchaser came in February, and made an enormous drop in the price he was giving for the rice that was to come: it was greatly to his advantage to buy the rice at that time and price, because in July he would get nearly six times as much for it.

The director of that factory had begun simply as a buyer of agricultural produce. By now he had several cars, several factories, and a lot of land. Francisco thought, 'This industrialist will soon be just like all the others; they become richer and richer at the expense of the poor, who become more and more destitute.' He was miserable at being so exploited, yet he had to sell the whole of his future harvest at that ludicrously low price, though the cost of living was very high, and the expense of stocking one's land for the shops in town made it impossible for the poor to save. Francisco was very much afraid of failure. He still had his rent to pay, and if he could not pay, he would be evicted. He still had to give his whole harvest to the man at the factory, so did not prepare any silo for keeping rice in. Yet he *knew* that the same rice he had sold for 1,500 cruzeiros he would soon be having to buy at 7,000 cruzeiros to eat, and to plant his next year's crop.

Their salvation was that Francisco's wife and daughters were marvellous workers, and helped to pay the family's debts by going to *quebrar coco* (open *babaçu* nuts). Then, one fine day, Francisco's eldest daughter was seduced by the son of the landowner. The young man had no intention of marrying a 'farm girl'. His father made an agreement with Francisco, and gave him a sum of money in compensation for the loss of his daughter's honour. Francisco's wife refused to accept any such agreement, and went to the judge; but she got no kind of hearing, because the *latifundiário* was a politician too, and both the commissioner and the judge were his friends. They simply suppressed the whole story, and there matters stood. Francisco was shattered by this series of events and wanted to move away ... but just think, *where* does one go with so large a family? Francisco's wife went one day into the forest to open *babaçu* nuts. She was attacked on the boss's land by his own *capangas* (these are strong-arm men kept by the *latifundiários* to inform on and beat the peasants, and even sometimes to burn down their houses and discreetly kill them). The *capangas* took away her axe, made various threats, and told her that if she wanted to open nuts there, she had to sell the nuts to the owner of the land who would give her half the recognized price, or else she could give him half the nuts.

Francisco meanwhile was concerned about the proprietor's cattle which kept getting into his land and destroying his crops. The landowner made no effort to prevent this. But Francisco himself could not even keep any animals, for he had no wood to make a fence, and the boss did not allow animals to wander free on *his* land. The only way to survive is to eat cassava flour with one's rice (which is very crude and has little nutritive value). It is flour made and sold as a sideline, for almost nothing. The proprietor had a kiln; everyone living on his land was obliged to dry their cassava in his kiln, and leave half the flour behind in the process. Francisco was annoyed too, because the *latifundiário* did not allow him to go to anyone else's shop, even though the shop on the estate did not supply everything the people wanted.

One day, Francisco's wife, who was pregnant, had a miscarriage from overwork, and very nearly died. Francisco could not afford to get her into the town to be looked after. He kept thinking, 'There are so many maternity homes and so many good doctors, but they are only for rich women; when will the wives of peasants be able to have such advantages?'

He saw all his children growing up without being able to go to school, not knowing even how to write their names. It made him deeply sad, and inwardly he was seething to see his children working so hard, and then not even able to celebrate the local festival, because they hadn't the shoes or clothes one needs to attend such a celebration. He was even ashamed for his children to appear in church in front of all the rich people.

One day Francisco spent a long time talking to a man who lived in an area where there was no road, and no bridge across the river, so people could travel only by boat or on horseback. As a result the farmers of that region had to sell their produce for whatever price the travelling buyers were willing to pay. Agriculture was very poor, and production was gradually going down. There were always all sorts of insects and vermin in the vegetables. After they had exchanged information about their various problems, this man pointed out to Francisco how, if he and all his fellow-workers united, they could improve their life, simply by

229

working together, and by putting the gospel into practice in their lives. After this conversation, Francisco gradually became more politically aware, and together with others in the area, began to decide that they could not accept things as they were.

He understood, and helped the others to understand, that they had value as human beings, that they were sons of God and not animals, created to live as free men, not slaves, and that God's earth was made for everyone, and not just for a few.

He began to meet with his fellow-workers; when they had a difficult problem to deal with, they would meet together to discuss what could be done. With these fresh activities and meetings, Francisco began to feel far stronger, and so did the others. He no longer felt the discouragement he had known before. He was no longer ashamed to go to church, and liked to listen to the priests defending the rights of the poor.

He discovered that the Church consists of all Christians who join in fighting against injustice, even though they may be persecuted by the rich. Francisco liked seeing priests and nuns among the peasants. In the past the peasants used to stay away from the priests, because the priests were friendly with the rich. They felt ashamed to face a priest, and did not find what he had to say to them any help in the daily struggle to live. Francisco felt that all this had changed since he had started those meetings. His fellow-farmers began to help each other much more with their work, and to improve their houses and the roads.

Thanks to the meetings of Rural Catholic Action, Francisco has already got together a group with the necessary courage and ability to demand justice and efficiency on the part of the authorities.

The spirit of friendship and cooperation among the people had enabled them to pay a teacher for their children. Francisco once thought only of getting away from the district, but now he says, 'If I go, my mates will be left in the lurch, unless someone else turns up to take my place.' So, he says, 'I shall stay; it will be difficult, but I will make myself fight to improve the situation of everyone else in my community.'

The latifundiários don't like Francisco because he has become 'politicized', and is now working to get his fellow-peasants into a union. He has great faith and great hope, and is prepared to fight the others even, if need be, to the death, to achieve their freedom.

The *latifundiários* forbade him to have meetings on their land, but that did not stop him, and he and his friends went on meeting wherever they could. It did not bother him that the landed proprietors tried to intimidate him and considered him a 'communist'. All he felt was, 'They consider the Pope a communist and the priests too, because they are enlightening the poor, and trying to help the poor to unite in their will to freedom. They treated Christ himself as a communist, after all, so why not me?'

One fine day, all the authorities conspired to catch Francisco out; they made up a story that he had stolen some cassava, and demanded that he either pay a large sum of money, or give up his land and go away. But he refused to panic, because he had not in fact stolen anything. A man whose conscience is clear is not afraid. So the police came to arrest him by order of the commissioner. Even Francisco's friends jeered, which made him very angry, but he did not give up just because of the disunity of one poor man criticizing another poor man so as to 'lick the shoes' of the rich and thus gain their approval. He saw it as a natural consequence of the exploitation and oppression of their situation.

While he was in prison, he thought, 'When it was a question of giving proof of justice and truth, Christ's disciples themselves gave witness.' And now it was up to him to continue Christ's work, to continue to foster the struggle for a better world, a new earth, to the point, if need be, of dying for his brother peasants. Finally he was let out of prison, and continued the fight. He had a clear conscience. He had made the discovery that the rich were trying to terrorize the peasants, so as to be able to keep them in slavery. But Francisco and his friends continued to fight hard for the liberation of their class, for that was what Christ had done.

His one wish was that all peasants should behave like Christ and not like Pilate, like brave men and not cowards.

After this account by Manuel (and all of it is true, but it would obviously be unwise to give the real names), came a succession of similar stories, and several farmworkers said in so many words, 'Francisco could be me...'

Having analysed the situation, and considered its underlying causes, the 110 people present at the meeting did some thinking about the meaning of human advancement in Christian terms, and the profound basis of their human dignity in God's design. Finally, they considered what kind of follow-up there should be to this meeting, what they could do now as a result of the things they had discovered together.

During the meeting, the farmworker members of the ACR decided to organize a *passeata* through the streets of C., to put their problems and sufferings before the general public, by means of placards and big inscriptions, and speeches. It was a great success. To make it clear that the movement was *not* communist (since we had been denounced as such to the federal police and various other authorities, who had telegraphed the local landowner not to allow us to use the areas we had planned for our demonstration), the eleven priests present for once put on their clerical clothes, and the *lavradoros* themselves decided to carry a statue of our Lady at the head of the procession.

The police kept a close watch on the whole proceeding, as indeed they had been doing throughout our meeting.

At present the state has three ACR centres, each comprising several teams spread over various villages. In February and March I shall be visiting those three centres with the area team, and organizing study days in each one.

The day after tomorrow, I shall also be taking part in a seminar on economic and social studies, and there are a lot of other things planned; in particular I want to make a small personal study of the area, which is required as part of my preparation for the chaplains' course I shall be going on in France.

So you can see that though I've left my job I'm not lazing about! I have 'left' the ACO too, for that matter, but only physically. In effect I shall be doing the same work with the ACR; it will be the same fight for the advancement of the poor; for it is clear that people in towns and those in the countryside must unite more and more and work together to bring about that 'liberation of man' which must come eventually.

Officially, I said goodbye to the ACO on Sunday 14 January, at a study day in P. during which Georges received 'popular sanction' for his nomination as diocesan chaplain of the ACO. It was deeply moving, and what made it more so was that each team made its own little farewell speech. The first to weep was Epifanio, a tough fellow of forty-five! After all, we're all human, and we have been working together since 1962, and have really got to know each other well. It's rather like a close-knit family – the ACO really is like my second family, and I believe I owe the fact that my priesthood has been happy, fulfilled and, I hope, faithful here largely to the team spirit and the need for authenticity and sympathy I have found in and through the ACO, among the poorest class in S.

It is already evident that Georges will do well as my successor – and Pierre too. Both are at present living in our old home in Santa Teresinha together with Richard, who is staying on there. It is not really a question of a new team being formed on our departure, but the first team becoming bigger, with very little difference: five of us will continue what three of us began (examination of our lives, sharing experiences and helping one another pastorally, pooling our money, etc.). We have decided to retain at least a monthly meeting among the five of us. There is some doubt as to precisely where in the interior Yves is to go, but we are waiting to hear. The archbishop has told me that I shall hear where I am being sent when I get back from France. In any case, Yves and I are both determined not to be limited to a little area, but to be at the disposal of the Church as a whole in the countryside, especially for work in politicizing base communities with the ACR for example, so as to achieve first a change in outlook and then a revolution in structures.

So there you are ... that's our news from S. There is still a lot I'd like to say, but we shall be able to talk about it all when I get to France, and how marvellous it will be to see you all! I only hope I won't be too much of a shock; you see I have become a bit of a Brazilian (though not as much as Yves) – and the trouble is always that one tends to adopt the bad habits and not the good ones – for example, arriving at meetings an hour late with no sense of guilt at all! Anarchy is only the exaggeration of a splendid quality which might easily vanish from the modern world – spontaneity (the mother of poetry?).

Thank God Brazil has kept that old 'graciousness'... A few days ago I asked Georges to tell me what had struck him most since he got here, whether among material things, or in our attitudes – and I bet you can't guess what he answered, 'The most striking thing is the *improvisation* that goes on.' I thought that was marvellous! So you can see what my own weakness is – but notice, he didn't say 'lack of foresight', but 'improvisation'.

This is certainly a long letter, and I've sweated over it, but I took advantage of a long rainy period which kept me stuck in the presbytery in Alcantara (with a great Canadian priest friend of mine). But it's also long because it is the last of a series. There will now be silence for several months, and then one day you'll get a letter from X. or Y. – some little town in the interior of the state; and another page will begin...

Part 6
The poorest are the most ready for God's word

LETTER

To his former parishioners and friends: For four or five hours the rain has been pouring down, and everyone seems to think it will last all day if not longer; so I'm making use of the time to write to you all again. I am back again in my 'home state'.

I left Paris from le Bourget on 13 January, and that evening we got to Dakar. From Dakar I went on to Keur Moussa, fifty miles away, where the Benedictines gave me a warm welcome; I spent a week seeing something of the African bush, and learning about the life and customs and problems of the people there. There is a lot they have in common with our people here, but a lot that is different too; I found it exciting to be in contact with 'Mother Africa' as I thought of her 'Brazilian daughter', for the coming of the black slaves, 150 to 200 years ago (especially in the north-east) made a profound difference to the whole of Brazilian civilization and culture. My eight days in Africa gave me much food for thought.

Arriving in Rio was like coming home after a short visit away. It was terrific to be back with the kindness, spontaneity and human warmth of the Brazilians. As the aeroplane stopped and we were all beginning to get up from our seats, the hostess asked us to sit down, and a health official came aboard, spraying us all generously with insecticide ... after fifteen minutes of this, presumably all our parasites and harmful germs were dead, and we were allowed to leave the plane.

In Rio the Assumptionist fathers I stay with are always most kind. And then there was the last stage of a splendid journey, and an emotional arrival in S. There were all my friends, priests and lay people, the same atmosphere, the same problems ... I felt as if I had hardly been away at all.

Everyone said how well I looked (the winter must have

done me good – I hadn't seen snow for six or seven years!).
My first call was at Santa Teresinha where I arrived to find
Pierre and Georges on the point of going to bed. The next day
I saw the archbishop and there were a host of other people to
greet and exchange news with... On 27 January, two days
after my arrival, the clergy study week began, a marvellous
chance to meet all the priests in the state again, and get back
into the swim of things.

Now I am to go to P., a little town along the railway between S. and T. (it's about 6½–7 hours from S.). I am delighted, first of all because there is work to do everywhere,
and the countryside is an enormous field of action where there
are massive problems, and people hungry for human and
Christian advancement ... and also because I know the area
slightly already: it is a very poor little town, but the people
are easy-going and friendly.

Finally, I am delighted because there will be (most important, this) a chance of priests and lay people working in a
group: the priests in several places nearby, three Brazilians
and two Italians, are determined to think out and put into
effect some kind of common action, and it is also the area in
which the ACR first began and is most firmly established.
There are fifteen or twenty little base communities which are
gradually becoming aware of their responsibilities, and they
are being visited and coordinated by two good leaders, Carlos
and Luís. Luís actually lives in P., where he is liked and
accepted by everyone as a leader; he will be able to give me a
lot of help as he has a profound knowledge of the whole
region, and of the problems, sufferings and hopes of the local
people.

So – I shall get to P. in a few days; Luís asked me to put off
coming for a fortnight so that he could prepare people to
welcome me, and for practical reasons too (he wants to put up
a little house of some kind as there is no presbytery).

I have taken advantage of the delay to take part in a course

238

on group dynamics (most interesting). I then spent several days in another town, working out plans for the ACR with Carlos and Luís and the local priest. Then followed a number of visits in S. – to the ACO leaders, the YCW, and various priests. Now I have come to M. (from where I am writing today) to visit the three French girls who have been here a fortnight now; they are doing health work, in the sense of education and advancement. They are in the process of setting up a little house in the middle of town, and I've been to give them a hand every day since I got here – except today when it hasn't stopped raining. They have themselves put together a kind of bamboo cupboard (an astonishing feat), and I take great pride in having made them a kind of wooden sink which will be useful for washing, doing the dishes, etc. They face an enormous task, but there are others already here to help and encourage them.

So that's my news, which will give you some idea of what I'm doing at the moment. I'll write properly when I've taken up my new job. This is merely to keep in touch... But I don't want to end without thanking all of you for the kindness and understanding you showed me when I was in France. Though it was sad leaving you, I have memories to give me the greatest support and encouragement in setting out on my new work. Greetings to you all.

P., *March* 1969

LETTER

To *his former parishioners and friends:* From now on you won't be getting your letter from S... In fact it is now almost two months since I moved to P., a small town in the interior of the province, and my life, my work, the problems I am facing, the people – everything is now totally different...

After being in S., the state capital, I find myself in the wide open country... P. is something over 100 miles from S., and I don't know whether to call it a big village or a small town. It certainly looks more like a village; I only wish you could be with me to see it. There isn't a single road with tarmac, or even stones; basically it is a group of houses (mostly straw or beaten earth) which have gradually been put up in the heart of a palm forest, linked to one another by what are no more than green pathways.

Since I got here I have not seen a single car or truck, for the simple reason that there is no way into P. by car.

Our only possible link with the world is the railway, built fifty years ago by an English company, during the time when Brazil's economy was no longer dependent on Portugal, had not yet become dependent on the USA, and was briefly dependent on England. An ancient, asthmatic, bone-shaking, puffing train is (despite all this!) the courageous link between P. and T., the capital of the neighbouring state, a distance of about 300 miles – the journey taking 15, 16, 17 hours perhaps, one can never tell in advance. Everyone knows what time the train leaves, but no one knows what time it will arrive! For instance, one Brazilian priest friend of mine promised to come to P. a few days ahead of me and get the place ready... I took advantage of the break to go to M. and give some help to the girls working there. What was my surprise, on getting back to S., to meet my friend, and to be told: 'You realize I never got to P.; I set off but never arrived, because the train left the rails, and we found ourselves in the middle of the *mato* (forest), miles from the station and then had to make our own way back as best we could. I walked a good way, and finally got a lift in a truck back to S...'

Note the difference: at home we say, 'the train was derailed', and this at once conjures up a major drama, or at least something unusual. Here, people are much more human; if you have an important call to make on your way, you let the stationmaster know and the train will wait for you, and if the engine 'leaves the rails' no one worries much, because we all trust the engine-driver to be able to cope with every eventuality, and we also trust in fate because 'there are plenty of accidents, but seldom is anyone killed.'

You should see the commotion at each station ... a crowd of children, women and grown men invade the train displaying and loudly crying their wares: birds, tortoises, chickens, snakes and every sort of animal, fruit, cakes, coffee, cold drinks, cassava flour, or the rudimentary self-service of platefuls of food...

At P., when the bell rings to announce that the train is about to arrive, a large part of the population come to the station: some to sell their meagre wares, but most of them simply to *see*, simply for the show. Yes, the isolation and poverty here are such that even the people themselves say that the train coming through (once a day, except Sundays) 'is the poor man's television'; and I must admit that I, too, am beginning to feel the same need to see something *actually moving*, simply in order not to feel stifled, shut in, a prisoner in a town to which no one comes, and which no one leaves.

There is an additional suffering one feels as a priest not only at being in a *place* with no life, no movement, but also at being with *people* who have no life and no movement – simply because they are unaware. They do not know. To give you one small example: the day before yesterday I visited a family. The mother was thin as a skeleton, visibly *worn out* by hunger, privation, poverty, sickness and one pregnancy after another; the (numerous) children were all pale and painfully thin but with the swollen stomachs that indicate worms, and one with the misshapen legs of vitamin deficiency; and yet, the mother was quite content with her lot, and felt that everything was fine with her and her family...

But let's get back to the beginning. I must first tell you how I arrived in my new 'parish'... Fr G., an Italian, was kind enough to come to P. ahead of me, and when they were ready he let me know. I got off the train to find an enormous crowd of people waiting at the station, all ready to hug me for joy,

241

with fireworks, flowers, compliments; then we had a stately progress through the streets of the town to the church (in ruins) and then the (temporary) priest's house: I went in pelted with rose petals... This is my Palm Sunday, I thought: afterwards will come the cross I must carry, and perhaps death to follow. There would be nothing surprising about it – such things have happened before. Meanwhile, why should I close my heart to the simple happiness of these poor and good people? For it is quite true that those who are poorest are often the most generous and most ready for God's word: the moment I got here I sensed a hunger and thirst for the gospel, the hope for some Message, some Presence, in these people to whom Christ has sent me. And as I came into this tiny, ruined church, I felt gripped by the most profound emotion; all I could say was, 'Yes Lord, it's all right. I am ready to be buried here. But I know I shall not die completely; I've come because you have sent me, and I am here to sow some seeds: it is better to start working slowly and in the dark (especially in these difficult times when priests and Christian leaders are being arrested as subversives), but whatever happens, if those seeds contain the vitality we know they do contain, and if the ground wants to receive them, then they will grow by themselves, they will spread on their own.'

Before I got here, the people had formed two commissions: one of young people, the other of adults. The first went from house to house to collect things the Padre might need. Everyone was ready to help, so that by the time I arrived I found all the basic necessities ready waiting: a hammock, chairs, a table, towels, rudimentary cooking equipment, etc. The adults had worked on the *casa do Padre* ... unfortunately, after a fortnight of back-breaking work to make the house habitable, the whole thing collapsed! But a widow offered to give up her house for a time and go to stay with her neighbour – which is how I come to be settled temporarily in this

242

little *casa* in the centre of the town. When I got here there was no shower or toilet – which is the case in most of the houses, but my neighbours assured me, 'It doesn't matter, Padre; after ten everyone is in bed, and you can go to the well and wash there' ... truly the simplicity of the children of God!

My first concern when I arrived was to get to know my new 'family'. You learn a great deal by visiting people in their homes. What struck me first, going through the different parts of the town, and crossing fields under cultivation and the *mato* (for the virgin forest is right on top of us here) to get to the more isolated houses, was on the one hand the tremendous richness of the soil, and on the other the intense poverty of the people. Every day I ask the same screamingly obvious question: 'Why? Why is the ground so rich, producing abundant rice, corn, beans, sugar cane, cassava and every kind of delicious fruit – and why, when you go into their houses, are you so appalled (every time, despite knowing the facts) by the sub-human life they live: straw or beaten earth huts, with one or two rickety stools, no form of sanitation, and no possible escape into any kind of happiness?' To me it remains a total mystery and a scandal...

The day I arrived in P., the man next to me in the train suddenly spoke to point out something from the window: 'See that *roça*? [*roça* = cultivated field]. Well it's the only *roça* alongside the railway between C. and S. ... I can remember, when I was young, there were lots of them; they were a pleasure to see. Now the whole thing has gone back to *mato* (uncultivated land, with only weeds or trees on it) because the *latifundiários* have gradually bought up – or taken over – the whole lot to enlarge their estates.' Just imagine a train in France only passing one cultivated field in 150 miles!!

One must not over-simplify: the poverty of the *lavrador* is the result of several factors; but undoubtedly the present agrarian régime is one of the major ones. Much is said at present about agrarian reform, since the passage of Constitutional Act 5, but the peasants are afraid that the *latifundiários*, who will be taxed in relation to the size of their estates, will simply make them foot the bill by increasing – as some indeed have already done – the rent for land, and the quantities of agricultural produce that must be handed over in proportion to the amount harvested.

And then there are the women who are forced to sell the *babaçu* coconuts to the *latifundiário* at less than half what he will sell them for. You can often see those poor souls going deep into the forest to bring down the *babaçus* with huge poles, and then bending over to crack them with an axe (and they are very hard indeed) to get the nuts out...

Almost never is there any money in the house: if people want to buy a tablet of soap, a little oil, or sugar, or salt, they have to go and break nuts. But everyone lives in a state of fear; you hear tales of this or that woman who tried to sell her nuts direct to the market, and when the landowner found out, he sent his *capanga* to beat her, take away her axe, etc. Often too, they are forced not merely to accept a ridiculously low price, but to give the landowners half their nuts for nothing !

In a few weeks' time (end of May, beginning of June), the rainy season will be over, and I shall begin my *desobrigas* – that is, my pastoral visits to the various villages that surround the town. Generally speaking, those villages are, as you can imagine, very isolated, and therefore even more primitive. There are many villages which the priest only visits once or twice a year, and many others where he never goes at all.

Around P., I have to make sixteen or seventeen *desobrigas*, generally four or five miles apart. The means of transport available are walking, riding, canoeing or taking a 'trolley', a little four-wheeled vehicle which travels along the railway lines, propelled by two men with things like big barge poles.

In P. itself we have achieved several gatherings of the people, to get to know each other better and become friends, and to enable people to say what they want their priest to do. For my part they have given me a chance to explain how I see my presence among them: that I want to be a kind of 'universal brother' who is part of the general community, and available for their service, together with what few possessions he has; who wants to help every individual to discover his own value (so often dormant or crushed out of existence) so that he too may be at the service of the community. Such is my sole ambition – but a big one. One idea which has come out during the course of these local meetings is the need for a smaller group that genuinely represents all the various strata of the population – made up, for instance, of one member of each occupation, chosen by his or her fellow-workers. Out of this was born what we call, perhaps too clerically, the 'parish council'; on it those who tend crops have three representatives (chosen by the group as a whole), cowmen one, railway-workers one, dockers one, masons one, carpenters one, cattle-breeders one, teachers one, mothers three, young people two, shopkeepers two. These representatives are not necessarily practising Catholics; all they need is to have the confidence of their colleagues, which is indication enough that they practise love of neighbour, which is what matters most in holding any community together. The parish is, after all, the community of the communities, of the families, the districts, the professions that go to make up a town. In practice, alas, it is seldom so, but that is basically what it should be; that is the dynamism of the gospel, the direction towards which we ought to be moving...

One of the council's first objectives was to rebuild the ruined church. But this will undoubtedly be succeeded by a host of other problems in the community to be dealt with as they occur by the group as a whole.

The young people have independently organized several meetings of their own. One practical result is in progress: they are forming a youth club. The idea grew out of their discovery of how isolated they are and how completely they lack organization.

Another enterprise that is of interest at present is the reorganization of our catechism classes. A group of eighteen young people (boys and girls) has agreed to take charge of all the children in the town on Sunday mornings in order to try to convey to them some minimum Christian vision. Every Saturday afternoon we meet together to think out and plan the Sunday morning's activities. In addition, the headmistress and most of the teachers have arranged to meet the Padre once a week to discuss their work as teachers, and see how they too may contribute to this awakening of a real religious consciousness in the children. I am finding all of this most exciting.

Holy Week included the washing of the feet of twelve *lavradores*, a simple but most moving ceremony, and a *via sacra* (way of the cross) through the town. The people had made a huge cross, weighing over a hundred kilos, and we called it 'the cross of hope', for, as I said to them, 'Jesus did not just die: he died and rose again. Does one say a wheat seed is dead? when a farmer has sown it, does he think he has sown death, that he has made the seed die? No, he has sown life, and multiplied life, and it is knowing that that gives him strength and hope and joy. So, too, our church – it is not just a ruin; it is crumbling, but is going to rise again... It is to show precisely this that we are all going to carry the cross of hope, and then set it up on the site of the old *and future* church.' It was in fact quite a sight to see. The young people provided the commentary for each station, and did the singing. And the different groups of workers were called in turn to carry the cross from one station to the next... *Lavradores, vaqueiros, ferroviarios, comerciantes*, teachers, carpenters, etc. When it came to the mothers, I must admit that I was worried: 'You're a fool, Paul. That cross is heavy! They'll never manage it; they'll fall!' I was all ready to call some of the men to the rescue, when we witnessed an astonishing scene : there was a real competition among the women – so much so that there wasn't room for them all, and the cross seemed to rise up and almost to fly like a feather over our heads! As we got to the tenth station, heavy clouds rolled up, and then it poured : that was the second point at which I worried a bit, thinking, 'Well, there we are; I'll be left alone with this cross like an utter idiot, and how shall I ever get it the rest of the way?' ... But my tears mingled with the falling rain as I saw that *everyone* was staying : there was only a second's hesitation, and the procession moved on, our clothes sticking to our skins, our shoes taken off to negotiate the water and mud better, and the singing only louder and more triumphant. At the last station, I invited the town officials to take their turn in carrying the cross : the Prefect, the treasurer, the police commissioner, they all joined in. The high point came when we reached the end; everyone got hold of a large stone, and in a moment the cross was upright, proud and firm, on its improvised pedestal. It was only a gesture, a symbol, but I felt : 'One may hope great things of people like this. Hope never dies (neither theirs nor mine). There is truth in the local proverb here : "hope is the last thing to die" – in other words, it still lives when everything else is gone.'

Otherwise, my dear friends, all goes well for me, physically and mentally. I'm in great form. My major difficulties at this point are :

1. The mosquitoes, fleas, horse-flies and other insects that bite. Never have I seen such hordes of mosquitoes. From 9 p.m. they descend on you in great regiments.

2. The isolation – by which I don't mean loneliness, which is something quite different : I am never alone. My house is full from early morning onwards. But is is simply a physical,

'biological' presence – the new priest is rather in the same category as the train going through. Here is something active, something moving, something to bring a bit of novelty to the drab horizon of lives which simply flow along, flow away, without ambition, from one end to the other, without purpose, without knowledge of the possibility of better things, without hope (or, rather, I am sure, with hope lying dormant).

At first, when people came to see me I would ask them, 'Is there something you want? Did you want to talk to me about something?' But no, they just come to *see* me, they stay sitting there for hours, just looking at me, not speaking, not really with anything to speak about. Once we have covered the subjects of the rain (heavy, light, frequent or rare), the crops (early or late), the animals (sick, or ready for slaughter by the butcher), there's nothing more to say. That is what I mean by isolation : starting from zero with these people who are very poor, quite uneducated, who know nothing of the world and have no idea what is happening to the rest of mankind at the moment, *even in Brazil*. Who can I talk to about Vietnam, about social problems, racial problems, the crisis in the Church, the May revolution in France, student unrest all over the world, capitalism, socialism, the Russo-Chinese conflict, Czechoslovakia, or anything else? I often try an experiment : even the children in the school cannot find this state on a map of Brazil, or Brazil on a map of the world. Speaking of maps : the other day I made one of the district (I love drawing, as you know), which I really need to help me get around the area and get to know it better. The next day about fifteen men came rushing into my house at seven in the morning with the Prefect at their head. I thought they must have some important message for me. But no – all they wanted was to look at my map ! They spent twenty minutes commenting on it with surprise and admiration as they found the name of each village : 'Yes, that's right – see, it's on the other side of the river', or 'Oh look, you can see where our river runs into the big river. How amazing !'

Please, all of you, continue to take an interest in the Third World and its problems. We must become brothers all over the world...

More about Penguins and Pelicans

The Pelican Latin American Library

The Twenty Latin Americas

Marcel Niedergang

Despite Bolívar's dream of a united society of Latin American states and the continental rhetoric of modern revolutionaries, the enormous land-mass lying between the United States and Cape Horn remains a political patchwork.

This two-volume work surveys some twenty independent Latin American republics from the geographical, social, economic and political points of view. In it Marcel Niedergang, the well-known journalist on *Le Monde* (who is an acknowledged authority on Latin American affairs), describes the countries one by one and gives details of their political organizations and national leaders and the degree of US and European economic penetration.

Volume 1 contains surveys of the following: Brazil, Argentina, Uruguay, Paraguay, Mexico, Guatemala, Honduras, El Salvador, Nicaragua, Costa Rica and Panama.

Volume 2 surveys Chile, Bolivia, Peru, Ecuador, Colombia, Venezuela, Dominica, Haiti, Cuba and the states of the Caribbean.

Cambão—The Yoke

The Hidden Face of Brazil

Francisco Julião

The yoke of an oppressive regime holds the peasants of Brazil to the land. Life expectancy is twenty-seven years, and starvation and torture form a part of everyday life. Yet from this demoralized group has sprung a force of bitter opposition.

Francisco Julião, a lawyer from the north-east of Brazil, who devoted his career to fighting corruption in that area, tells the story of the formation of the Peasant League in 1955. Thousands of desperate peasants braved intimidation to join him and the League became a powerful force. In this personal and moving account Julião details the objects of the League and describes its relationships with other resistance groups, the Church, the army, the trades unions and the regional authorities. In 1964 the movement was driven underground and Julião compelled to live in exile, but the League continues its struggle to lift the yoke from the people of Latin America.

Capitalism and Underdevelopment in Latin America

Andre Gunder Frank

'It is capitalism, both world and national, which produced underdevelopment in the past and which still generates underdevelopment in the present.' This study includes historical essays on Chile and Brazil, a discussion of the 'Indian Problem' in its relation to capitalist policy and an analysis of foreign investment in Latin America.

For the Liberation of Brazil

Carlos Marighela

A collection of writings by the man who, more than any other, shifted guerrilla opposition to Brazil's fascist regime into the towns. Practical and non-doctrinal, Marighela's papers, which were instantly banned when they appeared in France, can be read as a handbook for guerrilla fighters in Latin America and demonstrate how the struggle has developed since the death of Che Guevara.

* Not for sale in the U.S.A.

The Pelican Latin American Library

Guatemala - Another Vietnam? *

Thomas and Marjorie Melville

In this book two missionaries, whose ministry was terminated when they backed the cause of the landless Indian peasantry in Guatemala, describe the way in which the US government engineered the now notorious coup which brought an oppressive right-wing junta to power in place of the liberal government of President Arbenz.

Zapata and the Mexican Revolution †

John Womack Jr.

The definitive study of the legendary Mexican guerrilla hero, leader of a forgotten rural peasantry against the opportunist politicians of Mexico City, from 1910 until his assassination in 1919.

Also available

Brazil : The People and the Power
Miguel Arraes

Fidel Castro Speaks †
Martin Kenner and James Petras

Servants of God or Masters of Men?
The Story of a Capuchin Mission in Amazonia
Victor Bonilla

Guerrilla Warfare *
Che Guevara

Revolution in the Revolution? †
Régis Debray

* Not for sale in the U.S.A.
† Not for sale in the U.S.A. or Canada